A Short Guide to Shakespeare's Plays

JOHN GOODWIN

HEINEMANN
LONDON

Heinemann Educational Books Ltd
22 Bedford Square, London WC1B 3HH
LONDON EDINBURGH MELBOURNE AUCKLAND
HONG KONG SINGAPORE KUALA LUMPUR
NEW DELHI IBADAN NAIROBI KINGSTON
EXETER (NH) PORT OF SPAIN

ISBN 0 435 18371 0

Typeset by the Castlefield Press of High Wycombe
in 11/13 pt Baskerville, and printed in Great Britain
by Biddles of Guildford

Contents

*The plays in the order Shakespeare is generally
thought to have written them, although views
on this are contradictory and seldom precise*

For the author, this book is a small token of the work he shared at the Royal Shakespeare Theatre with A.C.H. Smith, George Mayhew and John Chilton.

Preface

The present age has been remarkable for a great renaissance of popular interest in Shakespeare's plays. It began in the late 1940s and early 1950s when a new audience, reacting against the austerities imposed during the war, took to the riches of Shakespeare hungrily. That enthusiasm has continually grown. There is now a public for the plays far bigger than at any other time in their history. The result is exceptionally powerful productions — sometimes so strong and original that they shift settled views about the plays themselves. But those views are volatile. They change the next time the same thing happens. Descriptions of key modern productions are not therefore featured in this book. It is written as a lasting guide, simply to indicate the story and general flavour of each of the plays. Its chief aim is to encourage people actually to see them in the theatre.

J.G.

Shakespeare: a Brief Biography

William Shakespeare was born in 1564, supposedly on 22 or 23 April, in Stratford-upon-Avon. His father, John, who was a prosperous glover there, preparing and selling soft leather, became alderman and later high bailiff.

Shakespeare was educated at Stratford Grammar School. When eighteen, he married Anne Hathaway — eight years older than he and already pregnant. Six months after the wedding their daughter Susanna was born. They had twins, a boy Hamnet and a girl Judith, two years later.

There are no records of Shakespeare's life during the seven years that followed, 'the lost years'. But by 1592 he was already an established actor and playwright in London.

He joined the Lord Chamberlain's Men in 1594, working as a leading actor and dramatist. By 1599 this all-male company of experienced and talented players — no women appeared on the stage until the Restoration — had built their own theatre, the Globe. Its owners were seven members of the company, including Shakespeare, who shared in its profits.

For the next decade the Globe, on the Thames at Bankside, was to be London's chief theatre, and the home of Shakespeare's work. Many of his greatest plays were written during these ten years, and were acted there. Both Queen Elizabeth, and after her James I, showed the company many favours.

In 1613, during a performance of *Henry VIII*, the Globe was destroyed by fire. But the Lord Chamberlain's Men, by now called the King's Men, had four years earlier leased a second, smaller playhouse, the Blackfriars. This was an indoor theatre, unlike the Globe which was open to the sky, and it had the technical facilities for scenic effects —

a fact which probably accounts for the spectacular element in Shakespeare's late plays.

In 1612, Shakespeare, it seems, went home. His son Hamnet had died when only eleven, but his two daughters were in Stratford with his wife Anne. He was now a wealthy man and had, as long before as 1597, bought a handsome house, New Place, the second largest in Stratford. It had two gardens, two orchards, and two barns. Here, with his family, he spent the last years of his life.

He remained friends with actors and poets, worked sometimes, and visited London. He bought a house in Blackfriars in 1613.

He died on 23 April, 1616, after entertaining Ben Jonson and Michael Drayton at New Place. He is buried at Trinity Church in Stratford.

He wrote thirty-seven plays.

[His is] a talent which more than any other the world has seen, reconciles us to being human beings, unsatisfactory hybrids, not good enough for gods and not good enough for animals. We are all Will. Shakespeare is the name of one of our redeemers.

Anthony Burgess

Titus Andronicus
(written possibly 1589)

TITUS ANDRONICUS, a play of barbaric ferocity, is rarely performed now, and the general belief is that Shakespeare wrote only a part. It was written when he was under twenty-five, and may have been devised by an actor and given to Shakespeare to improve, for there are passages which have his unmistakable mark.

Its theme, revenge, is acted out against the decadence of the disintegrating Roman Empire when the city was 'a wilderness of tigers'. Its characters are high-placed people who butcher each other in involuntary cannibalism. Kenneth Tynan describes the play as 'like Goya's "Disasters of War"', tragedy naked, godless and unredeemed, a carnival of carnage . . . the piling of agony on to a human head until it splits'.

The plot is macabre. The eldest son of Tamora, Queen of the Goths, is sacrificed to the gods by her Roman conqueror, the general, Titus Andronicus. She vows revenge. So her two other sons rape Titus's daughter Lavinia, and cut off her tongue so that she cannot say the names of those who raped her, and her hands so that she cannot write them.

Titus, also mutilated — his hand is chopped off — finds out the truth, and in turn kills Tamora's two sons and has them baked in a pie which he serves to her at a banquet. He then kills her and Lavinia, and is himself stabbed to death by Saturninus, the corrupt Emperor of Rome. Tamora's Moorish lover Aaron, a central figure in the crimes, is sentenced to be buried alive. The final massacre leaves less than half the original characters still living.

That this horrific play was a success with Elizabethan

audiences is conclusively recorded. It was given twice within ten days in 1594, sure evidence of popularity, and seventeen years later, in King James I's time, was noted as still a great favourite. Ivor Brown describes it as 'murder and rhetoric boiled up in a good blood-pudding . . . always an easy seller'. John Webster's plays, much liked in the early 1600s, were full of Borgia-like tortures, poisonings, graveyard murders, victims walled up or buried alive.

Titus Andronicus has been called 'a freakish Shakespeare rarity', 'a Shakespeare blood-bath', 'a grisly senseless map of horror' and 'the most notorious play in the Shakespeare canon'. But several remarkable and austere modern productions have caused critics to revalue the play's stature, and it is now sometimes considered partly a political allegory. A. V. Cookman writes: 'the atrocities are surely meant to illustrate the familiar Elizabethan metaphor in which the disruption of the body politic is imaged in dismemberment of individual men and women.' Trevor Nunn, who has directed the play for the Royal Shakespeare Company, says: 'Shakespeare pinned down in *Titus Andronicus* the Elizabethan nightmare. Even golden ages come to an end, in blood, torture and barbarism. . . . Appetite, the universal wolf, can usurp the throne of law. Rome, the greatest civilisation the world had known, had fallen . . . How could subsequent Empires, no matter how splendid, evade the same fate?'

The Two Gentlemen of Verona
(written possibly 1590)

Though there is no certain date for it, THE TWO GENTLE-
MEN OF VERONA could be Shakespeare's earliest comedy.
If so, it was written when he was in his mid-twenties. It is
about young people — their raptures, despairs, egotism,
idiocies, need for 'true' love, sudden desperate attach-
ments.

But its dancing language is not matched by a particularly
convincing plot or by compelling characters, and perhaps
for this reason it has seldom been popular.

There is no record of any performance until 1762;
even then it was staged in a considerably altered version.
Much later, it was still being ruthlessly adapted. Bernard
Shaw writes of an 1895 production as 'not exactly a comic
opera, though there is plenty of music in it, and not exactly
a serpentine dance, though it proceeds under changing
coloured lights. It is . . . a vaudeville.'

Since then, directors of Shakespeare's plays have come
to believe that it is on the whole better to trust his text,
not only with his masterpieces but also with his youthful
work — an attitude which often reveals unsuspected
strengths.

The plot of *The Two Gentlemen of Verona* is based on
a Portuguese novel, a pastoral romance. Greatly simplified,
it tells of the changing fortunes of two friends, Valentine
and Proteus. Valentine loves Silvia; Proteus loves Julia.
Proteus becomes infatuated with Silvia, thus betraying his
friendship with Valentine. Parallel to the adventures of
these two gentlemen run the adventures of their two
servants, Speed and Launce, and Launce's dog Crab. In the
end, the bond of friendship between Valentine and Proteus

is reaffirmed, and they are united with their original love-partners.

Whatever its shortcomings as a story, the play has wit, some lovely verse, a fresh experimental style, and one immortal lyric, 'Who is Silvia, What is she?'

There are, too, Launce's comic and touching soliloquies about his deplorable and loved mongrel, Crab. Herbert Farjeon writes that Charles Laughton had once declared to him that of all the characters in *The Two Gentlemen* Crab was the one he would most dearly love to play: 'Whereupon this amazing actor proceeded to give such a fine, such an adorable, sensitive and understanding performance of Launce's dog that I longed for Shakespeare to be there to see.'

But to audiences familiar with Shakespeare, the play's main fascination lies in the way it contains the seeds of ideas, themes, and characters that the dramatist was to make grow and flourish in later, more mature works: in, for instance, *As You Like It, Twelfth Night, Romeo and Juliet, A Midsummer Night's Dream.*

Caryl Brahms puts this element in *The Two Gentlemen* beautifully: 'A line here, and a situation there, speaks to the attentive heart like the voice of an old friend.'

King John
(written possibly 1590/1591)

KING JOHN is chronologically the earliest of Shakespeare's histories. It covers the period between the first year of John's reign in 1199 to the year after his death, 1217. England then had vast possessions in France. John —

the youngest brother of Richard I, Cœur de Lion — was in fact crowned not only King of England and Ireland, but also Duke of Normandy, Anjou, Maine, Touraine, and Aquitaine.

There is disagreement about the date of composition of *King John*, and about whether it came before or after another play on the same subject, author unknown, called *The Troublesome Raigne of King John*, a violently anti-Catholic work — which Shakespeare's is not, except for John's scornful denial of the Papal Legate's authority.

The plot deals with the see-saw of power between France and England, and concerns John's defence of his crown against the united Catholic powers of the King of France and the Duke of Austria, both of whom support the claim to the throne of Arthur, John's nephew, who is still a child.

Shakespeare shows in the play a cynical world where politics are what matters: expediency, or 'commodity' as it is described in a scathingly sarcastic speech. The characters are opportunists almost to a man, even killers, of the most inhuman kind, breaking truces and agreements with total indifference. Masefield says of John himself that, though clever, 'he is a traitor to his brother's son, to his own ideas, to the English idea, and to his oath of kingship.'

Doctor Johnson writes of *King John*: 'Varied with a very pleasing interchange of incidents and characters.' But he precedes this by saying it is 'not written with the utmost power of Shakespeare'. Anthony Burgess, among others, believes Shakespeare was working on the play in 1596 when he was filled with sorrow at the death of his only son Hamnet, aged 11. Burgess states '[*King John*] has fine lines, but the characters are pasteboard. And yet, knowing the special grief of the poet that summer we can find odd stabs of poignancy.' He evidences as most poignant of all the speech by Constance about her son Arthur, who is to die, beginning, 'Grief fills the room up of my absent child'.

King John is about political chicanery. But, ironically, it has a reputation for being a patriotic piece. This can only be because it contains some famous exhortations:

> This England never did, nor never shall
> Lie at the proud foot of a conqueror.

and,

> Come the three corners of the world in arms
> And we shall shock them; nought shall make us rue
> If England to itself do rest but true.

These last words — spoken by Sir Winston Churchill during the Battle of Britain — are the final words of the play. They strike a note sounded by Falconbridge, the bastard son of Cœur de Lion, who throughout the drama's action is a most satiric commentator on it. They come when King John's son Henry ascends the throne following his father's death, poisoned by a monk.

The Taming of the Shrew
(written early 1590s)

THE TAMING OF THE SHREW is perhaps the most famous play ever written about the battle of the sexes.

It tells how Petruchio, an adventurer, comes to Padua looking for a wife, and decides to try and win a young heiress, Katharina. What specially attracts him to her is not so much her beauty as that she has a reputation for scaring all suitors with her arrogance, anger, and violence.

Petruchio sees Katharina as an exciting challenge to his masculinity; he wants to subdue her: 'I will board her though she chide as loud/As thunder when the clouds in autumn crack'.

From the first, using clever, often brutal tactics, he is in command. He teases Katharina bawdily, pretends an excessive roughness, is totally unabashed by her blistering sarcasm, completely ignores the fact that she breaks a stool over his head, and takes her struggling into his arms saying 'Kiss me, Kate, we will be married a' Sunday'. Their consequent wedding, honeymoon, and eventual acceptance of each other in peace, make up a riotous but finally tender story.

As a foil to Katharina, fighting against the man she resists and then loves, is a second story, of Kate's apparently gentle younger sister, Bianca, who has a string of meek suitors. But, says Dr Johnson, 'The two plots are so well united that they can hardly be called two without injury to the art with which they are interwoven.'

There is also an induction, or prologue, sometimes cut, which seems to take place in Warwickshire. This shows how a tinker, Christopher Sly, is wakened from a drunken sleep, told as a hoax that he is a great lord who has lost his memory, and is installed in a rich bedchamber where, to entertain him, *The Taming of the Shrew* itself is performed before him, still drunk, by interlude actors — thus placing the action in a context that justifies its roughness. For it is, in fact, more a knockabout farce than a comedy. Anthony Burgess says 'it has a good playhouse reek about it'. Even so, there is a humanity beneath the surface that most modern productions try to stress.

The idea of a man moulding or taming a woman has been popular since the time of the Greeks; and the play, probably written before Shakespeare was thirty, is always enjoyed everywhere. Both *The Shrew* and Shaw's *Pygmalion* — in which Professor Higgins tries to turn a cockney flower-seller, Eliza, into a lady — were adapted into celebrated musicals: Cole Porter's *Kiss Me Kate*, and Lerner and Loewe's *My Fair Lady*.

At the end of *The Shrew*, Katharina makes a brilliant and moving speech, a complete volte-face, that some

15

husbands not only in Shakespeare's time but also today might welcome, and which a great many wives then, as now, would find exceedingly difficult to speak. At the centre of it is the thought: 'Thy husband is thy lord, thy life, thy keeper/Thy head, thy sovereign. . . .'

Romeo and Juliet
(written 1591 to 1596)

ROMEO AND JULIET is described on its title-page as a tragedy. But it differs in one major aspect from Shakespeare's supreme tragedies, *Hamlet, Othello, King Lear, Macbeth, Antony and Cleopatra*. In these, the heroes are destroyed through faults in their natures. Romeo and Juliet are innocent victims of destiny. They are parted by the hatred of their two families. The night she meets Romeo, Juliet cries 'Tis but thy name that is my enemy'.

But it is not this alone which destroys the lovers; the power of passion kills them too. 'Passion is destructive', writes Somerset Maugham, 'It destroyed Antony and Cleopatra, Tristram and Isolde, Parnell and Kitty O'Shea. And if it doesn't destroy it dies'. Coleridge says that 'all deep passions are a sort of atheists, that believe no future'.

Elizabethans were fascinated by the idea of passionate love. They delighted in it — and condemned it. Renaissance poetry, transcendently in Shakespeare's sonnets, brims with images of love shown, as in *Romeo and Juliet*, as a sweet-tasting fatal poison. There is another crucial point. W. H. Auden says 'It is impossible to feel the full tragic import of the play unless one can entertain, at least in imagination, the Christian belief held by everyone in an

Elizabethan audience, that suicide is a mortal sin, and that suicides go to Hell for all eternity. . . .' So when the lovers die at the end of the play, both of them by their own hands, they are immortally lost.

The story, says Anthony Burgess, is written with 'lyric fire'. It tells of the long vendetta between the families of Montague and Capulet in Verona. Romeo, a Montague, falls in love with Juliet, a Capulet, and secretly marries her. Juliet's cousin Tybalt challenges Romeo to a duel. Romeo refuses, but his friend Mercutio fights in his place and is killed. In anger and revenge, Romeo slays Tybalt, and is banished.

Juliet is commanded by her father to marry Paris, a nobleman; and the Friar who had secretly married Juliet to Romeo now helps her by giving her a potion which makes her seem dead. She is put in the family vault from where, when she wakes, she is to escape to Mantua with Romeo. But he mistakenly believes her really dead, goes back to Verona, kills Paris at her graveside, and then himself takes poison. Juliet wakes, finds her young husband's body beside her and stabs herself. The warring families, in grief, are reconciled.

The essence of Romeo and Juliet is that the lovers are doomed. It is ironic, and perhaps significant, that their names the world over have become a symbol of ideal youthful passion. To quote Anthony Burgess again: 'Shakespeare was thirty, perhaps thirty-one, when he wrote the play, and he was no longer young, but this of all works of literature eternises the ardour of young love and youth's aggressive spirit.'

Henry VI Part One
(written early 1590s)

The events in HENRY VI PART ONE plunge England into the Wars of the Roses, the bloody civil strife Sir Winston Churchill described as 'the most ferocious and implacable quarrel of which there is a factual record'.

As the play starts, Henry V is dead, and his crown is inherited by an only son, at first too young to rule. Because of this, and because the son, Henry, is weak, order is gone. France too has begun to rise up, lead against the English rulers by Joan of Arc, until she is taken and burned by the English as a witch. (Shakespeare's portrait of Joan, incidentally, is of a far tougher young woman than that presented 330 years later in the most famous play about her, Bernard Shaw's *Saint Joan*.)

Henry loses almost all the territory in France that his father had gained. But the story of *Henry VI Part One* is about the ruthless ambitions of the English nobles at home who fight amongst themselves for the power the King is too ineffectual to use. They eventually unite into rival packs. One of the great scenes is when the Yorkists and the Lancastrians stand in London's Temple Gardens disputing the rightful claim to the throne. The Yorkists pick a white rose, the Lancastrians a red, and in this brief, tense moment, the terrible civil wars begin.

To Tudor audiences the hero of the play was probably Sir John Talbot who was above the bitter hatreds of the warring Red and White Roses. A patriot and a magnificent old soldier who defeated Joan of Arc in battle, he dies when the quarrelling nobles in England fail to give him support on the French battlefields.

The character of Henry VI himself is shown as being,

though weak, also gentle, saintly (Henry was, in fact, considered for canonisation), and withdrawn from the violence of the battles.

When Shakespeare wrote the three parts of *Henry VI*, the history he broadly recorded was then only as distant from his audience as the first decade of the twentieth century is from us. Spectators no doubt enjoyed the immediacy, applauding in *Part One* 'brave Talbot', and responding enthusiastically to the battles, treacheries, plots, and counterplots.

Today the drama still grips, as it also does in *Henry VI Part Two* and *Part Three*, though all three parts are usually cut and condensed into either two plays or a single production.

Henry VI Part Two
(written early 1590s)

HENRY VI PART TWO, the centre of the *Henry VI* trilogy, is entirely about the civil strife in England during the Wars of the Roses. Most of the action is at the English Court, and shows the struggle for power brought on by Henry's weakness as a ruler — a struggle between groups of great nobles, the families close to the King. All were contending, says G. M. Trevelyan, describing the true historical situation, 'for power and wealth and ultimately for the possession of the Crown'.

The play opens when the saintly and young Henry first meets his future queen, Margaret of Anjou. He and the whole Court greet her with the words 'Long live Queen Margaret. England's happiness'. No words are to prove more ominous. For it is the fierce and subtle Margaret, later called 'the She-Wolf of France', who is to be the mainspring of Henry's tragedy, and of plots which John Masefield says were 'a welter of hate and greed'.

The first part of *Henry VI Part Two* concerns Margaret's schemes, with her lover Suffolk, to bring down the King's uncle and protector, Duke Humphrey of Gloucester, who has been Henry's good guide and counsel since he first ascended the throne as a child. Margaret, Suffolk, and the ambitious Cardinal Beaufort, first betray Gloucester, and then have him murdered. They achieve this by working with Richard, Duke of York, who also wants Gloucester's downfall. It is ironic that Margaret and York should plot together. Later they are to become the bloodiest of enemies, Margaret as head of the Red Rose faction, the Lancasters, and the Duke of York as leader of the White.

Meanwhile, there is a people's uprising, a 'ragged multitude of hinds and peasants, rude and merciless', led by Jack Cade who, although a peasant, declares himself to be Lord Mortimer, descended from the Duke of Clarence. This incident brings a certain lively relief to the sombre picture of bloody ambition at Court. But the rebellion – which was one of many plots against the King laid by the Duke of York – fails and Cade is killed.

Even so, York's power is rising. His treatment of enemies is savage: he has Suffolk banished and then slain. One by one, the House of Lancaster are removed so that he can reach the throne. And he is strongly supported by the mighty Warwick, the famous 'Kingmaker'. The play ends with the first triumph of the House of York, at the battle of St Alban's, when Margaret and the King are defeated.

The play, though complicated, is strong and hypnotic. It skilfully weaves together a pattern of ambition and betrayal, plots and bloody murders, with each character fully drawn, a living being.

Henry VI Part Three
(written early 1590s)

In HENRY VI PART THREE, the final play in Shakespeare's trilogy about that war-torn reign, Henry is deposed by the Duke of York, and finally murdered by Richard of Gloucester, the hunchback Duke who later becomes King Richard III.

Throughout the trilogy the relationships of the warring nobles, their ambitions and retributive hatreds, are intricate and shifting and could easily be tedious in the hands of a lesser writer. Peter Hall, who directed the play as part of the celebrated *Wars of the Roses* cycle for the Royal Shakespeare Company, writes: 'Shakespeare recognises that good men can become bad kings, that good politicians may have to do evil', and that quarrels seldom have right on one side. Because of the dramatist's profound understanding of this, he makes the whole savage struggle a gripping chronicle of power and how it can corrupt.

The final play of the three starts by showing how Henry, deposed by York aided by Warwick the 'Kingmaker', begs to continue reigning for his lifetime, but is willing to resign the crown to the York faction at his death. His Queen, Margaret, and the young Prince, their son, are filled with shame at this act of disinheriting the House of Lancaster. The wars that ensue favour first one side, then the other.

At a particularly brutal battle, Margaret and the Prince win a victory in which many of York's followers are slain and his young son butchered. Margaret, her 'tiger's heart wrapt in a woman's hide', takes York prisoner and gives him a napkin to wipe his eyes which is drenched in his dead son's blood. She taunts him before she has him beheaded.

Close on this scene of powerful horror comes Henry's

famous and beautiful soliloquy on the battlefield when he laments the weight of kingship and the anguish of war: 'Oh God! methinks it were a happy life/To be no better than a homely swain. . . .' A man enters carrying an enemy he has killed, and discovers it to be his father. Then another enters in the same way, and discovers he is carrying his son. The King, the father, and the son weep together.

At a later fight Henry loses his crown and is made prisoner by York's son who becomes King Edward IV. Edward is the antithesis of the defeated King. He is a magnificent soldier, a proud, pleasure-loving, lustful man, surrounded by his family, yet unaware that his own brother Richard, the hunchback Gloucester, already plots to have his crown.

The new King Edward offends Warwick, who in revenge drags Henry from his prison in the Tower and makes him King once more. But Edward, in the battles that follow, is victorious, and the hunchback Gloucester stabs Henry to death in the Tower.

The play ends with Edward again enthroned and rejoicing with his Queen and their young Prince. He is all unconscious of his brother Gloucester's plots. 'Here', he says, 'begins our lasting joy'.

Richard III
(written 1592/3)

The events in RICHARD III, though possibly distorted by an exuberant and politically-aware genius, were very real to his audience. There must have been people who saw the original performances whose grandparents had actually lived during Richard's reign.

Chronologically it follows the *Henry VI* trilogy which, in the last part, shows the start of the hunchback Duke of Gloucester's progress to England's throne. In *Richard III*, by judicious plots and murders, he reaches the Crown, only finally to be slain on Bosworth Field.

Much of the play can be enriched for the audience if they have seen Shakespeare's previous histories in sequence. The characters of Richard himself, of his brother Edward IV, of Edward's Queen, of old Queen Margaret now diminished to a Cassandra, embittered and almost mad, are all more understandable if they have been followed through the preceding years and shifts of power.

Despite this, *Richard III* has always been popular on its own, and the reason for its fame is undoubtedly the central figure. He is an extraordinary conception: deformed from birth, his arm withered, his nature murderous, with no gleam of humanity, but much satanic and sardonic humour.

The part is often successfully acted as a flamboyant royal cut-throat, more comic than repulsive. Colley Cibber began this in the eighteenth century, playing an 'improved' *Richard III* which audiences gleefully enjoyed, relishing such interpolated excesses as Richard's 'Off with his head! So much for Buckingham!' about his one-time friend and chief helper to the throne.

Garrick, Kemble, and Kean all carried on the tradition of making Richard an alluring monster, and though Irving returned to Shakespeare's text, he too showed the character as a magnificently entertaining villain. Laurence Olivier's legendary performance on stage and film was the climax of this particular reading. More recently, in the shadow of Hitler and Stalin, the play has been difficult to present without some apprehension of modern history.

Richard III is crowded with characters, and its patterns of Court relationships, old griefs, and new murders, come together as a chronicle of glittering fascination. The moment it opens we get Richard's resounding speech beginning: 'Now is the winter of our discontent/Made glorious summer by this sun of York. . . . '

But the play is more than a theatrically effective portrait of a villain. It shows the end of the Wars of the Roses; the end of an era of power politics at their most bloody. And it concludes with Richmond's victory over Richard at Bosworth: a symbol of the order and peace that was to start in England with Henry VII, the first of the Tudors.

It is now believed that Shakespeare's Richard differs much from the actual king. A. P. Rossiter writes: 'To think that we are seeing anything like sober history is derisible naivety. What we are offered is a rigid Tudor *schema* of retributive justice and a huge triumphant stage personality . . . a monstrous being incredible in any sober historical scheme of things.'

Debate about the 'real' Richard III has always thrived. He is thought by some to have been sensitive, intellectual, even handsome. He almost certainly was not deformed and had no withered arm. Rumour of the murder of the little Princes in the Tower — the heirs of Richard's brother and predecessor as King, Edward IV — agitated the public for centuries, though the murders were never proved.

But Richard has never lived down his reputation for using ruthless means to get to the throne. And Shakespeare's superbly mercurial devil, the 'abortive, rooting hog,' has a lasting hold on the public's imagination.

Love's Labour's Lost
(written not later than 1594)

LOVE'S LABOUR'S LOST shows a group of adolescent, high-spirited men and girls, playing at love and playing with words.

It is a study in artifice, expressed with wit and elegance. But the fact that it contains a fair amount of Elizabethan quibbling, obscure references, and in-jokes, makes its verbal subtleties not easily accessible to twentieth-century audiences, though some modern productions have brought it ravishingly to life.

It was probably written for private performance in the garden of some Tudor manor, only later being revived for the public. It has very much the flavour of its time, responding to the current literary fashion — an essentially Elizabethan delight in words. Nearly every character is involved in a kind of inspired word-game.

'In its deftness, richness, neatness, delicacy of quip and swiftness of retort,' writes John Masefield, 'it seems as ingenious as cobweb, but the sun of today does not shine upon it as the sun of the great Tudor time. Then, it was a way of writing that none could neglect, that all esteemed, and were moved by. A mind so sensitive as Shakespeare's, interested in every way of writing, could not fail to be moved by a way so skilful and so new.'

The story itself is about the youthful King of Navarre and three of his courtiers who swear to fast, pray, and study for three years, completely giving up the company of women. Almost at once they find they are forced to break their vow. For when the Princess of France and her Court arrive to discuss state matters, the King falls in love with the Princess, and his three courtiers with her ladies.

This leads to much deception and mockery.

Near the end, however, there is a famous and, in the context of the fun, jarring interjection of mortality. The Lord Mercade arrives to tell the Princess that the King her father is dead. 'Suddenly,' John Masefield says, 'the world of fantasy is broken up by the news of Death. There is no make-believe about Death.'

And finally at the very end, after all the elaborate invention and brilliant artificialities, comes one of Shakespeare's best known poems: one concerned with life as it is really lived. He describes the 'daisies pied and violets blue' of spring, and, in winter, the icicles that hang by the wall, the milk frozen in the pail, and greasy Joan keeling the pot.

E. M. Tillyard writes of this: 'Even in so stylized a play, where the theme is as much the words men use as the lives they lead, Shakespeare comes to rest in the norm of everyday life, and specially in the country life that in those days preponderated in England, with the shepherds piping in spring and the girls bleaching their frocks against the summer, and in winter the coughing in church and Tom bearing logs into the hall of the Great House.'

The Comedy of Errors
(probably first performed 1594)

THE COMEDY OF ERRORS is a title which exactly describes the play. The plot, most ingeniously contrived and extremely intricate, chiefly concerns the adventures of two pairs of twins (two masters and their two servants) who are constantly confused for each other. Nearly every scene adds a new and inventive twist to this theme of mistaken identity.

It was written when Shakespeare was under thirty and his own twins, Hamnet and Judith, were small children.

The story, says John Masefield, 'showed for the first time in our theatre a lively sense of the natures of women'. In the main it is the kind of comic entertainment which has been popular for hundreds of years, though there are here and there a few faint shadows which, as in all Shakespeare's comedies, are absorbed into its 'healing and regenerating wholeness' (John Wain).

The action is set in Ephesus, noted in the ancient world for the study of magic and spells, a town 'full of cozenage/ As nimble jugglers deceive the eye/Dark-working sorcerers that change the mind'.

Elizabethans loved *The Comedy of Errors*. A performance in 1594, just after Christmas, was so packed and rowdy that the next day a mock enquiry was held about its revelling audience. Ten years later, also as part of the Christmas festivities, it was presented before King James I's Court.

In the eighteenth century, writers and actors apparently wished to 'improve' it: various versions appeared with such titles as *The Twins or Which is Which*, and *'Tis All a Mistake*. Shakespeare's own play was restored to the theatre in 1865 by Samuel Phelps. It has often been set to music, was once sung as an operetta, and Rodgers and Hart wrote a musical version, *The Boys From Syracuse*.

Shakespeare's principal source was a play over 2,000 years old, *Menaechmi*, by the Latin dramatist, Plautus. Clifford Williams, who directed a production of *The Comedy of Errors* for the Royal Shakespeare Company which was seen throughout Europe and America, writes: 'Plautus loved scurrility, gagging, backchat, topical allusion, and obscenity. His style was boisterous, his characterisation coarse ... [But] Shakespeare was a dramaturgical alchemist. All his life he filched ingredients, prescriptions, and formulae, and never failed to transform them. He is never less than honest to the vivacious bawdry of his Roman mentor, but the crude, jolly and essentially pagan *Menaechmi* is tempered in the flame of Christian humanism. . . . Shakespeare gives us a crazy though magical Ephesus where men may re-find their brothers and find themselves, and where women may re-find their husbands and learn about themselves. The city and people of Ephesus may be highly improbable, but they are infinitely desirable; a triumph of imagination over life.'

A Midsummer Night's Dream
(written c1594)

A MIDSUMMER NIGHT'S DREAM is a brilliant play about magic. In Shakespeare's time, it was his marvellously rhythmic and evocative words, expertly acted on a bare wooden stage, that communicated that magic. But the scope the story offers for spectacle has, over the centuries, tempted many producers into lush extravagances, musical as well as scenic, sometimes with the full Mendelssohn score, a huge cast, and about half Shakespeare's text.

There is now, though, a strong and growing movement towards restoring the play that was written, with a balance between effect and simplicity. Peter Brook who directed for the Royal Shakespeare Company a radical and famous production in a plain white setting, writes: 'Today we must open our empty hands and show that really there is nothing up our sleeves.'

28

It is likely that the first performance of *A Midsummer Night's Dream* was to celebrate a noble wedding, of the Earl of Derby to Elizabeth Vere in 1595, with the Queen and the entire Court present. According to Anthony Burgess, comedies at that time largely depended on the falling-out of lovers. 'But', he continues, 'to have such a falling-out motivated by failure of affection in the lovers themselves, or indeed produced by any human agency, would be indiscreet in a wedding piece, so Shakespeare introduces the fairies' — who, adds Burgess, are 'tough and dangerous demons more than figurines in ballet shoes, not essentially malevolent but, to use the theological term, uncovenated powers'.

The play starts with Theseus, Duke of Athens, speaking with impatient love of his forthcoming marriage with Hippolyta. It ends four days later with the wedding night, at which an unwittingly comic interlude, in the form of a so-called tragedy, *Pyramus and Thisbe*, is acted by Bottom the Weaver's group of rustics to entertain the bridal pair.

The time between is concerned chiefly with the adventures of four Court lovers. Hermia and Lysander leave Athens because their love for each other is opposed, and are followed to the woods by Demetrius who also loves Hermia, and Helena who loves Demetrius.

There, Oberon, King of the Fairies, angry with his Queen, Titania, and wishing to punish her with a trick, commands Puck to fetch for him a magic juice which, dropped into sleepers' eyes, makes them fall in love with the first being they see when they wake up. Bewitched by this juice, Lysander falls in love with Helena, and Titania falls in love with Bottom, whose head Puck has transformed into the likeness of an ass.

When Oberon's wish to punish Titania and Puck's liking for mischief are satisfied, the spells are lifted. The lovers are united with their true partners, and Bottom and his company speed to the Court to act their wedding night play.

No doubt, the enduring popularity of *A Midsummer Night's Dream* is to some extent due to the fact that two potent enchanters, love and magic, are the mainspring of its action. Few people during the 400 years since it was written can have agreed with Pepys' verdict: 'The most insipid ridiculous play that I ever saw in my life.'

The Merchant of Venice
(written 1594/5)

THE MERCHANT OF VENICE has always been enormously popular, partly for its love story, partly because it blends the universally absorbing themes of love and money ('flesh and gold' says Anthony Burgess), but mainly because it contains a great theatrical protagonist, Shylock, the most famous Jew in all literature.

Shakespeare had at least two contemporary sources for the character of Shylock. One was Christopher Marlowe's play *The Jew of Malta*, a success at the time. The other was the notorious execution at Tyburn of Doctor Roderigo Lopez, a Jewish physician who had attended Queen Elizabeth.

Lopez had fallen out with the powerful Earl of Essex and, despite the Queen interceding for him, was condemned to death on a fabricated charge. At his execution he cried: 'I am a Christian and I love the Queen.' The crowd shouted, 'Hang him — he is a Jew!' A vivid demonstration of racial attitudes in Tudor England.

When Shakespeare was alive Venice was the most

glittering of all merchant cities, a gorgeous image of cosmopolitan money-making. A drama in which 'the willing, generous, and prosperous transactions of love's wealth are compared and contrasted with Shylock's wholly commercial transactions' (John Russell Brown), could not be set in a more appropriate place.

The story tells how men from all over the world travel to Belmont to woo Portia. He who chooses, out of three offered caskets — made of gold, silver, and lead — the one that holds her portrait, may marry her.

Amongst these suitors is Bassanio, a Venetian who, impoverished by prodigality, raises the money to go to Belmont through his friend Antonio, the merchant of the play's title. Antonio has himself borrowed the money from Shylock and guarantees the loan with a pound of his own flesh — a bond regarded as a joke.

Bassanio falls in love with Portia and she with him, chooses the right casket, and marries her.

Meanwhile in Venice, Antonio cannot meet his bond to Shylock because his ships and treasure have been lost in a storm. Shylock claims the pound of Antonio's flesh. Bassanio leaves Belmont to rescue Antonio, and Portia follows him disguised as a lawyer. In the courtroom she wins the case for Antonio. Shylock is fined and humbled.

The play concludes on a note of lyrical romantic comedy, shared by the lovers and Shylock's daughter Jessica, who has left him and married Bassanio's friend. At the end, too, Antonio's ships are reported saved.

With the greatest commercial city of the time as his setting, Shakespeare makes this fact rub off on to every main character. Portia is wealthy, which is one reason why she has many suitors. Bassanio has squandered his own money, which is why he looks for a rich wife and why he has to borrow. Antonio risks his fortune, even his life, on his ships and cargoes. And Shylock uses his wealth for an attempted revenge on the Venetians whom he hates for their eagerness to borrow from him while still insulting him.

Certainly the sympathy of the audience is more often with him that with his enemies. 'He is honest in his vices; they are hypocrites in their virtues' says Hazlitt on Edmund Kean as Shylock. It is true of the character as well as of Kean's way of presenting it.

As with all great roles, the part invites many different portrayals. Modern performances have shown both a spiteful, fawning creature of the ghetto, and a Shylock who was a noble, misjudged, and suffering man.

Richard II
(written not later than 1595)

Shakespeare wrote ten history plays in all. Eight of them — *Richard II*, the two parts of *Henry IV, Henry V*, the three parts of *Henry VI*, and *Richard III* — follow one another chronologically. Together (though complete in themselves) they unfold more than a hundred years of English history, and trace the bloody and unstable period from Richard II's deposition and murder, to Richard III's defeat at the battle of Bosworth Field.

RICHARD II, the first in this sequence, is about a king's fall. But it is more than a crown that is taken. The idea of divine right, and medieval belief that a king was appointed by God and was therefore God's symbol upon earth, until then unquestioned, is also violated. Anyone who rose against the anointed King, or even so much as countered his wishes, was considered to be committing heresy.

Shakespeare's Richard is shown as a vain man who has built up in the English Court an indulgent, intensely self-regarding and enclosed world of flatterers. But though absolute ruler, he is weak, whereas his cousin Bolingbroke, whom he recklessly exiles because of a quarrel, is strong. Bolingbroke is the 'new man', ruthless, ambitious, not afraid of the Godhead of the Crown. Returning to England with an army to reclaim his lands and wealth, he pays lip service to the concept of kingship whilst, in the interests of 'good government', climbing steadily up the ladder of ambition, finally to reach its top — Richard's throne. For the unbelievable happens, and 'the deputy elected by the Lord' is deposed. The King is turned into a subject.

Richard takes a kind of exquisite melancholy in his own fall, in his own destruction. Shakespeare gives him some of the most beautifully elegiac speeches in all drama. And at the end, in prison, a few moments before he is murdered, his words 'I wasted time, and now doth time waste me' echo the whole of his tragedy.

Richard II has a particular power, not only as a work of art in itself but as the catalyst of Shakespeare's sequence of history plays. Just as Orestes was haunted in Greek drama for offending the gods, so it is with the assassination of Richard and the assumption of his crown by Bolingbroke, who becomes King Henry IV. The men who committed the double crime of regicide and treason, though they believed their motives were just, cannot throw off an anguished guilt at what they did. And their expiation of that crime leads to the bitter and terrible Wars of the Roses, between the houses of York and Lancaster — descendants of Richard and Bolingbroke.

Henry IV Part One
(written 1596/7)

Bolingbroke, who took the King's crown in *Richard II*, is King himself in HENRY IV PART ONE. His deposition of Richard plagues him with guilt. To expiate it, he longs to lead a crusade to the Holy Land. But his people at home are uneasy and rebellious. Even some of those who helped him to the throne have turned against him. And his son, the young Prince Hal, spends his time living riotously with dissolute friends, preferring them to his austere father and the Court.

Hal's companion in loose-living is Sir John Falstaff, enormously fat and a huge drinker. Hal calls him a 'vast bombard of sack', recognises him as a rogue and a clown, but nevertheless regards him at this time as a kind of substitute father.

'A self-indulgent, impotent whoremaster, a thief, a liar, a cut-purse, a cheat, a braggadocio, in love with himself and his own company, immensely and seductively attractive.' That is Falstaff according to the directors of the play — Peter Hall, John Barton, and Clifford Williams — when it was staged as part of the complete history sequence presented by the Royal Shakespeare Company at Stratford-upon-Avon in 1964 to mark the 400th anniversary of Shakespeare's birth.

Falstaff indeed represents the world of the senses. But W. H. Auden has written: 'We become aware, behind all the fun, of something tragic. Falstaff loves Hal with absolute devotion . . . he believes that his love is returned, that the Prince is indeed his other self, so he is happy, despite old age and poverty. We, however, can see that he is living in a fool's paradise, for the Prince cares no more for him . . . than he would care for the King's jester.'

For Hal's jokes hide a darker, more serious, maybe less attractive, side of his character. He truly relishes the pleasure of Falstaff's company. But he draws experience from the fat knight's humanity. He is preparing for the time when he will be King. He must know the people, and know himself, if he is to govern.

As admired for his courage as Hal is castigated for drinking and whoring, is Hotspur, the choleric son of the Earl of Northumberland. Hotspur and his father raise a rebellion against Henry IV, claiming the right to England's throne of Hotspur's brother-in-law, Edmund Mortimer. Civil War has begun. The rebellion brings Hal to his father's side: he joins the King, and it is Hal who meets Hotspur in battle and kills him.

Henry IV Part One is partly a study of kingship devitalised, showing how a country divides when its leader is flawed. It also shows kingship in training — the young prince Hal seeking knowledge of life outside the Court. But the most alluring parts of the play are perhaps all Falstaff's. He is Shakespeare's greatest comic creation: a vision of human frailty that makes us laugh. He radiates sardonic humour, self-mockery, high spirits, human weakness. William Empson speaks for the world as well as Prince Hal when he writes: 'To love Falstaff was a liberal education.'

Henry IV Part Two
(written 1597/8)

The mood of HENRY IV PART TWO is of age and decay. When it opens, King Henry, who in *Part One* ruled a country split by bitter civil wars, is sick in mind as well as body, guilt-ridden at usurping Richard II, his past glories nothing to him.

His son Prince Hal, in *Part One* temporarily reconciled to his father, fighting for him during the Earl of Northumberland's rebellion, has returned to Falstaff and the rogues and whores of Eastcheap. A fresh crop of conspirators, this time led by the Archbishop of York, plot a new insurrection under the banner of religion. England, like its King, is torn by struggles springing from the deposition of Richard.

King Henry suffers, as well, from the absence and what he believes to be the permanent loss of his son. But the Prince has begun to change. He sees that life with Falstaff and his companions represents nothing which can uphold or strengthen a country; rather that which can only destroy — disease, lying, stealing, vice. There is no doubt in this play that Falstaff will lose the Prince's love.

But Falstaff fascinates us still. The shadows, though, have begun to fall. The man who is described by W. H. Auden as 'untiring in his devotion to making others laugh' cannot clown forever. He feels age and illness. In a celebrated scene, which in its tone anticipates Chekhov, he and Justice Shallow reminisce in an orchard, talking of their lost youth, of their friends 'all dead', of the passing of time, and of their boyhood escapades when 'we have heard the chimes at midnight'.

Meanwhile, the King is dying. At his deathbed, father and son are at last united in understanding. The crown, the 'polished perturbation! golden care' with its weight and its guilt, passes to Hal. He accepts it as a 'living and moving responsibility'.

Then at the end of the play comes the necessary separation from Falstaff. Hal does it brutally, perhaps feeling there is no other way. At his Coronation procession through the streets he is approached by Falstaff who is joyful at the Prince's accession and expects royal favours. Hal rejects him at once: 'I know thee not, old man: fall to thy prayers; How ill white hairs become a fool and jester. . . .'

Hal has no time for Falstaff now. He is sufficiently experienced in the ways of men, and in self-knowledge, to try to restore order and good government.

The Merry Wives of Windsor
(written 1597 or later)

The word 'merry' in the title of THE MERRY WIVES OF WINDSOR is apt: not only for the Windsor wives but for the play itself, which is more a romping farce than a comedy.

It is traditionally thought to have been written by Shakespeare at great speed, some say in a fortnight, to meet the command of Queen Elizabeth who had been so delighted with the character of Falstaff in the *Henry IV* history plays that she wanted to see the fat knight again — and in love. There is a well supported theory that the play's first performance was before Queen Elizabeth at a Garter Feast at Whitehall Palace in 1597.

The Merry Wives is Shakespeare's only comedy to take place in England (Italy or France or imaginary countries like Illyria provided settings for the others). Another rarity is that all the main characters except Falstaff are not aristocrats, as was usual in Shakespeare, but ordinary folk, up to anything in the way of fun. They are part of a new and growing middle class, wealthy and aspiring but with peasant roots. Karl Marx found 'in the first act alone more life and movement than in all German literature'.

Few serious commentators have shared Marx's liking for the play. But it has always been immensely successful with audiences (and with composers — Verdi and Vaughan Williams have both made famous operas from it).

The story, which happens against a background of English country life, it seems in winter, comes from no known source. It has the elements of many popular comic plots, and is full of tricks, practical jokes, misunderstandings.

Frank Ford and George Page are wealthy citizens of Windsor. Sir John Falstaff, badly in need of money, approaches both their wives, who plot together to punish him by playing on his lust for Mrs Ford. They give him three opportunities to be alone with her, though in fact they intend to make a fool of him.

During the first, alarmed at the approach of Ford who arrives insanely jealous, Falstaff hides in a dirty clothes-basket and is tipped from it into the Thames. During the second, again scared by the arrival of Ford, who is again madly jealous, Falstaff escapes dressed as an old woman. Finally Falstaff goes to a village frolic in Windsor Forest disguised as Herne the Hunter, but is pinched, mocked and scorched by 'fairies' carrying long lighted candles.

At the end, all is forgiven, Ford is cured of his jealousy, and Page's young daughter, wooed through the play by three men, gets the one of the trio whom she loves.

It may or may not be true that Queen Elizabeth had,

in fact, asked Shakespeare to write her another play about Falstaff. What *is* certain is that the knight's return to the stage did not give the Queen, or us, quite the same man as in the *Henry IV* histories. William Hazlitt writes: 'His wit and eloquence have left him. Instead of making a butt of others, he is made a butt of by them.'

But Doctor Johnson believes that the play's 'general power is such that, perhaps, it never yet had a reader or spectator who did not think it too soon at an end'.

Much Ado About Nothing
(written 1598/1600)

Beatrice and Benedick may not be the heart of MUCH ADO ABOUT NOTHING, for many think it lacks one, but they are certainly its spirit.

Beatrice, attractive, forthright, is — so she declares — a happy and confirmed spinster. Benedick, a man's man and a soldier, maintains that a bachelor's life is the only life for him.

But between them — though they will not admit it, even to themselves — is a fiery mutual attraction. This they express by constantly provoking and teasing each other. And in their duel of words, sexual at root and often very witty, lies the play's lasting power to amuse and engross an audience.

Intertwined with their story is another rather unreal one which tells how Claudio, Benedick's friend, is about to marry Hero, Beatrice's cousin, but is deceived into believing she has a lover. In a dramatic scene, Claudio denounces her in church at their wedding; she faints and is taken away as dead; and this causes Beatrice and Benedick, serious for once, to be drawn together in a close alliance by their intense concern at what has happened.

The end of the play shows Hero recovered, proved innocent, and united again with Claudio; Beatrice and Benedick happily tricked into admitting their love for each other; and the two pairs dancing into marriage.

The story is counterpointed by characters of another kind. These are the comic, bucolic members of the Night Watch who by chance clear Hero of Claudio's accusation. Their chief is a gorgeously self-important ass called Dogberry. He is one of Shakespeare's funniest creations, relished by Elizabethans and still loved today.

But *Much Ado* remains, in essence, Beatrice and Benedick, particularly Beatrice. John Dover Wilson describes her as 'the first woman in our literature, perhaps in the literature of Europe, who not only has a brain, but delights in the constant employment of it'. She is, without a doubt, a star amongst Shakespeare's heroines, themselves the most marvellous gallery of female characters ever invented.

Benedick glitters too. And the entertainment value of the loving quarrels between him and Beatrice started a dramatic tradition. Plays by Congreve, Wilde, Bernard Shaw, Noel Coward, and others, have all used the same situation, though Shaw, who invented a similar wrangling pair in *Man and Superman*, actually castigates Shakespeare's originals. He writes: 'The main pretension in *Much Ado* is that Benedick and Beatrice are exquisitely witty and amusing persons. They are, of course, nothing of the sort. Benedick's pleasantries might pass at a singsong in a public-house parlour. . . . Precisely the same thing, in the tenderest degree of her sex, is true of Beatrice. . . . There is only one thing worse than the Elizabethan "merry gentleman", and that is the Elizabethan "merry lady".'

But even Shaw finally admits the play's magic: 'No

matter how poor, coarse, cheap and obvious the thought may be, the mood is charming, and the music of the words expresses the mood.'

Shakespeare, 'the sexiest great writer in the language' (A. L. Rowse), was in his middle thirties when he wrote *Much Ado*. And his instinctive, because pre-Freudian, understanding of how strong sexual feeling can affect surface behaviour is evident in the play's two principal figures. It is they (and Dogberry) who more than anything else, have ensured its success from the very beginning.

Henry V
(written 1599)

After the disturbances following Henry IV's deposition of Richard II, HENRY V shows a time when England is one again, ruled strongly by the man who only a short while before, as Prince Hal, had spent his youth drinking and whoring with Falstaff in Eastcheap.

Henry V's father on his deathbed had advised him 'to busy giddy minds with foreign quarrels'. The King, perhaps because of this, starts a war with France. It successfully unites his subjects in a common patriotic venture.

With the miracle of the Battle of Agincourt, Henry becomes in the eyes of his people the picture of Edward Hall's description of him a century later: 'the blazing comet . . . the mirror of Christendom and glory of his country.' His victory against a far bigger French army resulted, according to Shakespeare, in the loss of only a few English nobles and 'of other men/But five and twenty', whilst the French losses are 'ten thousand'.

But Henry, an astute politician, brings the two countries together afterwards by wooing the Princess of France as his Queen.

The story of *Henry V* is exciting, moving quickly from England to France and to the battlefield. The French are shown as extravagant, vain, boastful; the British as soldierly, brave, eccentric.

Partly as a consequence, the play is thought by many to be not much more than a marvellously effective drum-and-trumpet show, heightened by some superlative scenes. But when this tone matches the current feeling of the audience, as in a time of war, it can be heartening and full of hope. Laurence Olivier's film of *Henry V*, made in 1944, was enjoyed by an immense public who were then enduring hardship.

Shakespeare, however, surely had more than a jingoist view. *Henry V* is not merely a hymn to a country's pride and to its young king-hero. Peter Hall, who directed the play as part of the Royal Shakespeare Company's complete history sequence in 1964, writes: 'We see what it was actually like to be in the field with Harry, cold and wet, in fever and fear, boredom and pain . . . The play's tension is between these two extremes: it is a red and golden land of hope and glory at Agincourt, but also a place of hacked limbs and putrid corpses.'

The character of the King appears equally ambivalent. He is the man who inspires his troops by assuring them of the eternal glory of being present with him in battle: 'We few, we happy few, we band of brothers. . . .' He is also the man who, the night before, has passed disguised through the tents of his soldiers talking as one of them, and sharing their fearful and common humanity.

Henry V is without doubt a celebration of war. But it is a criticism of war too.

Julius Caesar
(written possibly 1599)

Since Shakespeare wrote JULIUS CAESAR it has been continuously popular. Bernard Shaw, though impishly critical of many of its aspects, calls it 'the most splendidly written political melodrama we possess'.

The play, which keeps to the broad outline of history, shows Caesar at his zenith, a colossus bestriding the world. But he appears only in a few scenes. The dramatist's main concern is with the nature of those who for mixed motives assassinate him, and the avenging destiny which follows and destroys them once their fatal action — taken, they claim, to save Rome from an ambitious tyrant — has split the city into opposing factions, bringing war.

Shakespeare presents Caesar as a man heaped with triumphs, who is vain, superstitious, easily flattered, and believes his own legend. He even challenges the sacred Roman principles of Republican liberty by desiring the Imperial crown offered him.

There is convincing factual evidence of this side of Caesar. For instance, the Roman historian, Suetonius, reports that he accepted honours 'which as a mere mortal he should certainly have refused'.

Moving against Caesar in the play, as in history, are Brutus and Cassius, the leaders of the conspirators. Shakespeare invests them both with extraordinary depth and humanity. Brutus, like Hamlet, is given the character of an anti-hero, a thinker, an idealist, a man of self-doubt. Cassius, his friend, is in many ways his opposite — restless, passionate, pragmatic, fiercely jealous of Caesar's power. It is Cassius who works on Brutus until even he, 'the noblest Roman of them all', believes that to kill Caesar is morally right. 'Let's carve him as a dish fit for the gods', Brutus says to his fellow conspirators the night before the assassination. He wishes for a ritual sacrifice in the Capitol, the justifiable destruction of a great but too powerful man, done only to give freedom back to the Roman people.

Next morning Caesar, who at first has hesitated to go to the Capitol (his wife has dreamed of evil portents and begs him to stay at home), is finally persuaded to do so. Once there, he is butchered almost immediately. Each conspirator springs forward and stabs him. Brutus' knife is the last of all.

Now another marvellously drawn character becomes a force: Mark Antony. Hearing of the assassination he rushes into the Capitol to find Caesar, his loved and loving friend, dead and bleeding.

It is at this point that Brutus makes the first of his mistakes. He underestimates Mark Antony, senses no danger from him, and agrees to allow him to give Caesar's funeral oration on the condition that he, Brutus, talks to the people first. Brutus handles the confused and excited Romans coolly. He explains clearly and logically why Caesar had to die. His arguments are well received. He then publicly gives Antony permission to speak.

But Antony, the sensualist and soldier, is more than he seems. Standing beside Caesar's body, he speaks the most famous funeral oration in the world, beginning 'Friends, Romans, countrymen'. Cleverly, he does not use any logical appeal to the people. With the understanding of a man who himself lives more by his body than his brain, he deliberately inflames the mob to unthinking physical action, to a frenzied hatred of the conspirators.

Antony's great speech is the trigger for the wars that follow. He and Octavius, Caesar's nephew, lead an army against Brutus and Cassius, between whom there are bitter quarrels. Finally, Cassius, his troops defeated, kills himself.

Brutus, haunted by the apparition of Caesar, and also defeated, kills himself too. Murdered Caesar is avenged.

As You Like It
(written c1600)

AS YOU LIKE IT is one of Shakespeare's best loved comedies. John Russell Brown writes of its 'light-footed gaiety, warmth, and confidence'. The play's heroine, Rosalind, is a superb creation: sensitive, subtle, ardent, intelligent.

It was written during the late part of Elizabeth's reign. There was then — perhaps as a reaction to the commerce and change of the time — a vogue for pastorals, a wish, in the words of the play, to 'fleet the time carelessly, as they did in the golden world': most of the action of *As You Like It* takes place in the Forest of Arden.

Before the story begins, a good Duke, usurped by his ruthless brother Frederick, has taken to the forest with a few faithful courtiers. They live there simply, happily, and in freedom, though sometimes hungry, and chilled by the harshness of men and weather.

Rosalind, the good Duke's daughter, has remained at Court to be with her friend and cousin, Celia, Frederick's daughter. She sees a well-born young man, Orlando, win a wrestling match in the palace, and falls in love with him at sight.

But soon afterwards she displeases Frederick who banishes her. Disguised as a boy, she leaves to search for her father in the forest, taking with her Celia and the Court jester, Touchstone, a worldly man with a zest for life. Orlando, separately, leaves for the forest, seeking refuge from his brother, Oliver, who treats him cruelly and has withheld his inheritance.

It is at this point, soon reached, that we come to the pastoral heart of the play with its changing and elusive moods. Everything that gives *As You Like It* its exquisite quality happens in the forest, which provides hospitality and love in contrast to the animosities of the Court.

Orlando, meeting Rosalind in the forest in her disguise, believes her indeed to be a boy. She suggests that, as a game, he should pretend to woo her. Out of the restraints imposed by this highly artificial situation spring love scenes unmatched in their mixture of lyricism, passion, irony, and fun.

Before the play finishes, all the exiles have met together, and all the love affairs are happily resolved — not only that of Rosalind and Orlando, but of Oliver, for instance, who follows Orlando to the forest and is captivated by Celia. As in all happy endings, the rightful owners get back their possessions.

But *As You Like It* is more sophisticated than appears from a description of its simple plot and enchanting love story. It beguiles audiences because of the complex attitudes and relationships of its characters; because it eloquently argues the difference between life in the country and life at Court; and because it balances an exuberant idealism with canny realism. From time to time, too, as a counterpoint to the prevailing rustic innocence, some bitterly humorous notes are sounded by a melancholy cynic of some charm, Jaques, one of the banished Duke's courtiers. High born, he relishes his own sourness in the rustic world. It is he, a solitary among the woodland love affairs, who speaks the over-quoted descant on man's decay, beginning: 'All the world's a stage/And all the men and women merely players. . . . '

Twelfth Night
(written c1601)

TWELFTH NIGHT is often called the most perfect of all Shakespeare's romantic comedies, of which it is the last. Written just before the great tragedies — *Hamlet, Macbeth, Othello, King Lear, Antony and Cleopatra* — it is a bridge between the two forms, comedy and tragedy, and contains elements of both.

There is almost incontestable evidence that it was first performed at Court on 6 January 1601 to entertain a Tuscan Duke, Orsino, during his official visit to Queen Elizabeth.

The action of the play takes place in a land whose very name, Illyria, has come to mean romantic, fairytale happenings. For Elizabethans, its title alone stood for the traditional feast of liberty, a saturnalian revel, at which the world was turned upside down and the usual rules of conduct were reversed. Twelfth Night's sub-title is 'What You Will'.

The main story concerns Viola who, shipwrecked and thinking her twin brother drowned, disguises herself as a boy, and becomes page to the lovesick Duke Orsino of Illyria, carrying his messages of entreaty to the Lady Olivia whom he adores unrequitedly. Olivia, in turn, falls in love with Viola, thinking her a boy. Viola herself falls in love with the Duke. At the play's end, Viola marries the Duke, and Olivia marries Viola's twin brother who has returned, saved, from the sea. The events that lead to these marriages carry a prevailing atmosphere of highly-charged longing, of painful, youthful love in a golden land.

A darker note is touched by the other characters, who are neither young nor particularly happy, and who have recognisable human vices. Sir Toby Belch is a wit and a gentleman, but he is also a drunken rogue who does not think twice about taking his friend Aguecheek's money in return for falsely promising him Olivia, his niece. Aguecheek himself is good-natured but weak, silly, and a coward. Olivia's steward, Malvolio, the play's central comic figure, is a self-important, cold man, 'a kind of Puritan'.

There are no happy ends for them. Aguecheek is fooled and left without his fortune; Sir Toby is badly beaten over the head in a fight and marries a waiting-maid he doesn't love. Malvolio fares worst of all: for the sake of a cruel revengeful joke by Sir Toby and his cronies, he is locked in the dark and treated as a madman.

Standing between the ideal romantic world and the cold light of day, between the Illyrian lovers and drunken Sir Toby with a bandaged head, is Feste, the clown, the 'allowed fool', who sings of the wind and the rain, and the melancholy passing of time:

In delay there lies no plenty;
Then come kiss me, sweet and twenty,
Youth's a stuff will not endure.

Hamlet
(written 1601/2)

HAMLET has fascinated the world since it was first staged. It has been performed more than any drama ever written. Quotations from it have become part of our language. 'It is one of mankind's great images', writes Peter Hall who has directed the play for the National Theatre and the Royal Shakespeare Company. 'It turns a new face to each century, even to each decade. It is a mirror which gives back the reflection of the age that is contemplating it.'

Laurence Olivier writes of Hamlet the man: 'He is the permanent rebel and nay-sayer, and would be the same in any society or period of history. He works out his morality as he goes along, taking nothing on trust, and approaches life like an actor, always trying on new characterisations to see if they fit.'

Hamlet was written when Shakespeare was in his middle thirties and is the first of his great tragedies. The legend from which he drew his story goes back to an eleventh century Icelandic poem. The play is, in fact, a 'revenge' drama, a genre very popular at the time. The theme of these was always basically the same. The central figure is committed to revenge a great crime, and his subsequent actions usually bring darkness, self-doubt, suffering and finally death.

The plot of *Hamlet* tells how Claudius has poisoned his brother the King of Denmark, Hamlet's father, taken the throne, and married Hamlet's mother, the Queen. Hamlet sees his father's ghost, who demands that he revenge the crime by which he was 'of life, of crown, of Queen, at once despatch'd'. The great part of the play then deals with Hamlet's efforts to do this. He swings between indecision and resolve, fiercely rebukes his mother, and stabs to death the father of the girl he loves, Ophelia, who then goes mad and, wandering by a stream, drowns.

At the end, Claudius plots for Hamlet to be killed in a duel between him and Ophelia's brother, Laertes, who agrees to use a rapier with an envenomed point. During the match, Hamlet is pricked by this but its effect is slow, he continues to fight and, while scuffling, he and Laertes change swords. Laertes is mortally wounded, and the Queen, unknowingly and fatally, drinks from a poisoned cup prepared for Hamlet in case he is not cut by Laertes' rapier. Hamlet senses treachery. At last he finds the impetus to kill the King. Then he too dies.

It is a strong story. But what gives the play its extraordinary depth and appeal is the complicated and ironic character of Hamlet himself. The best-known soliloquy ever written, starting 'To be, or not to be', spoken when he considers taking his own life, expresses the agonising indecision that is only a part of his nature. The speech, revealingly, concludes: 'Thus conscience does make cowards of us all/And thus the native hue of resolution/ Is sicklied o'er with the pale cast of thought.' It is Hamlet's racing brain and imagination that wreck his purpose.

The play is widely accepted as Shakespeare's masterpiece. Its ambiguities will continue to be discussed for as long as man exists. Perhaps, as John Dover Wilson thinks, we were never intended to reach the heart of its mystery. Paul Scofield, a notable modern Hamlet, feels 'there is something inviolate in his character which is proof against analysis and labels'.

Certainly, self-identification is a factor. Coleridge writes, 'It is we who are Hamlet'.

Troilus and Cressida
(written 1601/2)

TROILUS AND CRESSIDA is a profound and sardonic but discordant work. John Barton, who has directed the play twice for the Royal Shakespeare Company, writes: 'Shakespeare doesn't impose a uniform tone; he offers a jarring mixture on all levels: characterisation, text, plot and action. This structure is a deliberate and organic orchestration of dissonances.' At the time it was written Sir Walter Raleigh considered it 'the despair of all critics who seek in it for unity of purpose and meaning'. Recent productions, though, have revealed it as an undoubted masterpiece with an immense theatrical impact.

One clue to its present-day success can be glimpsed in a statement made by Bernard Shaw in the 1890s. Deriding the public of that period for craving, in the theatre, fantasy rather than reality he adds: 'Shakespeare made exactly one attempt, in *Troilus and Cressida*, to hold the mirror up to nature; and he nearly ruined himself by it.' It could be argued that theatregoers in the second half of the twentieth century are responsive to the play precisely *because* it has an awareness of stark reality. A. P. Rossiter's point also rings home to us today: 'We can see in *Troilus and Cressida* codes of conduct, standards of values, and ethical principles all standing on trial.'

What Shakespeare does is to focus with fierce and devastating criticism on his two constant and primary concerns, love and war. He mocks the warrior heroes of legend while decrying the folly of romantic passion and castigating the horrors of battle.

The setting is Troy towards the end of the ten-year seige waged by the Greeks to get Helen back to her husband, Menelaus, one of their kings. She has been seduced and taken to Troy by Paris, a Trojan prince.

All the main characters, except Cressida, are from Homer's *Iliad*. Cressida and her love affair with Troilus derive from a poem by Chaucer, itself a remodelling of earlier works.

The plot tells how Cressida, a Trojan girl, desires and is loved by Troilus. Her uncle Pandarus brings them together. They become lovers, but are parted the next morning when she is delivered as a hostage to the Greek camp, outside Troy's walls. She is at once unfaithful with a Greek commander, Diomedes, and Ulysses leads Troilus to where the

51

two of them are together so that he can witness for himself her quick betrayal. Later, Hector and Troilus fight the Greeks. Hector is barbarously slaughtered by Achilles and his Myrmidons. Troilus tries to kill Diomedes but fails; fails also to kill himself; and curses Pandarus who brought him Cressida.

To a great extent the story seems to be used by Shakespeare as a frame in which to place his thoughts. There are, for instance, two magnificent dialectical speeches spoken by Ulysses — one on Degree and its place in men's conduct, the other on Time and its effect on men's deeds. These have a brilliant and enduring philosophic force. Throughout the action, too, the play's events, its wanton women and war-sickened men, are bitterly and obscenely commented on by a kind of scabrous chorus figure called Thersites who intensifies the dramatic argument.

The play has no tragic hero; no noble death at the end, with hope springing for a new order after the evil has gone; no king or dominant figure is carried slowly on to a high stage for the people to mourn. Yet the great humanist, Goethe, says 'Would you learn to know Shakespeare's unfettered spirit, read *Troilus and Cressida*'.

All's Well That Ends Well
*(date of composition very uncertain:
possibly 1602/3)*

Without exactly saying why, most literary comment defines ALL'S WELL THAT ENDS WELL as a 'problem play'. It is certainly a challenging work to stage, possessing a formidable heroine, a hero difficult to warm to, and a curious story. But it can be extraordinarily fascinating.

It is neither comedy nor tragedy. Nor does it belong with the late romances, for its tone is not similar. It is sometimes grouped amongst the dark comedies, such as *Measure for Measure*, but its shadows are lighter, and its brightness more pervading.

Yet it is this very ambiguity which gives *All's Well* its special interest — though as far as the public is concerned, that interest has seldom been strong. Now, however, it is finding favour. Stuart Hall writes that it has something 'irretrievably modern' about it.

The theme concerns a woman asserting herself against male prejudice and stupidity. The story shows how Helena, a physician's daughter who has been brought up by the widowed Countess of Rousillon, comes to Court, and with one of her late father's prescriptions heals the King of France of a fistula. As a reward, he promises that he will use his power to enable her to marry the man of her choice. She chooses Bertram, the Countess's son, with whom she is passionately in love.

Bertram is furiously indignant at being forced to marry a commoner, and declares he will never be her husband until she gets the ring he wears, and is pregnant with his child: in other words, until the apparently impossible happens. He then goes off to the wars in Italy, hoping never to see her again.

But Helena follows him in disguise, and by secretly taking the place of another woman, a whore, in his bed (the 'bed-trick', much used in medieval and Renaissance stories), she makes him her unknowing lover and at the same time gets the ring.

At the end, returned to the French Court, the wars finished, Helena reveals what has happened, confronts Bertram with the ring, announces she is carrying his child, and they are reconciled.

Though Bernard Shaw believes the Countess to be

'the most beautiful old woman's part ever written', the play in most ways is Helena's. And despite the fact that her resourcefulness twice puts the man she adores in an intolerable position, Coleridge claims that 'Shakespeare's consummate skill interests us in her' and makes her 'his loveliest character'. Shaw too writes of her 'sovereign charm', no doubt finding her very like his own forceful female characters.

Bertram, on the other hand, has nearly always been considered unattractive. Doctor Johnson says 'I cannot reconcile my heart to Bertram; a man noble without generosity, and young without truth.' But in Bertram's defence, it can be argued that to have a wife thrust upon one to settle the King's medical bill might be thought burdensome.

A different kind of dominant male figure in the play is Bertram's companion at the wars, Parolles: a grotesque boaster, brimming with brave talk, but terrified when the danger is actually around. Charles I was so amused by the swaggerer that the play in his time was retitled *Parolles*.

All's Well concludes with a feeling of general happiness. Helena has Bertram who promises to love her. The Countess has her son back from the wars. Even Parolles, who has been made to look a fool, finds at last some honesty and declares himself 'simply the thing I am'. So all is *almost* well. It has been said that the title should finish with a question mark.

Othello
(written 1603/4)

The theme of OTHELLO is sexual jealousy. The story has no sub-plot — rare with Shakespeare — and takes the main characters swiftly and inexorably towards destruction. To see this is like watching a storm growing: first the sky shows only one ominous cloud, but this quickly spreads bringing darkness and violence.

The plot, from a sixteenth-century Italian novella, centres on the Moor, Othello, an honoured Venetian general who, as the play opens, has married Desdemona. But the mainspring of the action is Iago, one of his officers. Disappointed at not being promoted, this ingenious and totally evil man is resolved on revenge, both on Othello and on Cassio, Othello's lieutenant, the rank Iago covets.

In Cyprus — a Venetian possession which Othello and his army have been sent to defend against a Turkish fleet — Iago's revenge begins.

He contrives for Cassio to be dismissed from the army by making him drunk. He then, through the great middle scenes of the play, goads Othello into believing that Desdemona is Cassio's lover. Othello is enraged by unjustified jealousy. He strangles Desdemona. Iago's wife finds out her husband's plot and discloses it. In an agony of remorse, Othello kills himself. Iago stabs his wife to death and is arrested.

The immense force of the drama is partly because it is about a universal emotion, jealousy. Also, the events take place in a domestic and private setting, rather than one opened out to wider concerns. And the time-span of three nights and two days is more compressed than in any other Shakespeare tragedy, giving the story a pitiless intensity.

Othello is not young, and of an alien race to Desdemona. Yet she is as passionately in love with him as he with her, perhaps because of his strangeness. She has absolute confidence in Othello's love and as absolute an ignorance of his vulnerability. She is a double victim: of Iago's lies, and of her husband's capacity to believe them.

Iago is an enigma: the motives that drive him to revenge seem inadequate to the tragic conclusions of his actions. Yet, watching, one is seldom conscious of this. Iago's vitality and strength make their own truth. He never repents.

The language of the jealousy scenes, and of the Moor's last speeches, are a cataract of wild abstract images — 'word-music' in the phrase of Bernard Shaw, who believes that attempts to make literal sense of these parts of the play should be forgotten, and the voice used only as an instrument.

Anne Barton describes the almost unbearable nature of the story as it pushes on to an inescapable catastrophe: 'The cast of characters is small, the atmosphere fevered and claustrophobic, and the passion under analysis — sexual jealousy — particularly painful and humiliating. Most of the action takes place at night, in a darkness sinister in itself which gradually becomes an emblem of the incomprehension, ignorance, and self-delusion of the characters. . . . Not by accident, *Othello* has a long history of audience intervention: of performances in which someone, forgetting that it is only a play, has stood up and tried to warn Othello against Iago, or to proclaim Desdemona's innocence.'

Measure for Measure
(written c1604)

MEASURE FOR MEASURE is a strongly-spiced and sensual mixture of high principles with lustful and questionable actions. It is about justice in relation to sexuality, and the abuse of authority by those in power. It places these themes in a corrupt Vienna of leprous prisons and seething brothels.

Sexual feeling is strongly evident in much of Shakespeare, and this play expresses it fully — so much so that in the middle and late nineteenth century it was thought indecent and seldom performed.

It is, however, one of the writer's most original dramas, and can still provoke controversy, though this is now more likely to be concerned with its ambiguities than its capacity to shock.

Its sombre tone and sour humour show Shakespeare moving from the dazzling enchantments of most of his previous work into an altogether different world. *Measure for Measure* was part of the dark mood which only lightened with the final romances, and which gave us the tragedies of *Othello* and *King Lear*, the ferocious misanthropy of *Timon of Athens*, and the intense sexual cynicism of *Troilus and Cressida*.

Over that period, maintains Ivor Brown, 'The sun sank sharply in Shakespeare's sky. The pettiness of man and the frailty of woman began to obsess his imagination.' Both are evident in *Measure for Measure*.

The story, based on an event said to have actually happened in Italy in the Middle Ages, tells how the Duke of Vienna leaves on a mysterious absence, instructing the strict, seemingly cold Angelo to govern in his place.

Angelo, sickened by the sexual licence in the city, promptly enforces an old law making fornication punishable by death.

The first to be condemned under this law is Claudio, whose love, Juliet, is pregnant ahead of the wedding. Claudio's sister, Isabella, goes to Angelo to beg for her brother's life. Angelo, the declared enemy of sexual passion, is overcome with lust for her. He promises to free her brother if she will give way to him.

Isabella, who is about to become a nun, is full of horror. She tells Claudio in prison what has been demanded of her. Claudio entreats her to do as Angelo asks. But Isabella still refuses: she is in a kind of religious exaltation and cannot sacrifice her virginity even to save her brother's life.

The missing Duke meanwhile has remained in Vienna, disguised as a friar, secretly observing how Angelo rules. He persuades Isabella to pretend to consent to Angelo — her place in bed to be taken in the dark by Mariana, a girl Angelo was to marry and has deserted. This bed-trick makes Angelo believe he has made love to Isabella, but he afterwards orders that Claudio shall be put to death just the same.

In the final scene, the Duke emerges from his disguise; Angelo's crimes are revealed; Claudio is re-united with Juliet; and Isabella first shows a miraculous mercy by successfully asking that Angelo's life be spared, and then accepts the Duke's proposal of marriage. Angelo himself is commanded to take Mariana as his wife.

The most vivid character in the play is Angelo. But to many, the Duke is of equal or more interest. He is an enigma who has been both admired and scorned. G. Wilson Knight writes that he 'holds within the dramatic universe, the dignity and power of a Prospero'. Others, including Hazlitt, consider the Duke slightly ridiculous, more interested in himself than in the feelings of others. John Wain has described him as a 'contriving, sermonizing waxwork'.

Isabella's chastity-at-all-costs attitude had some support at times when an extreme morality was the fashion. But the idea has irretrievably lost ground.

Macbeth
(written c1606)

MACBETH was written about the time when Europe was obsessed by the idea of witches, a feeling intensified in Britain by King James I who had just published a study of demonology.

Among Shakespeare's dramatic works, it alone is wholly concerned with evil; and among Shakespeare's great tragic figures — Hamlet, King Lear, Othello, Macbeth — the last is the only one damned. Many disasters have accompanied the staging of the play: so much so that some actors believe it can itself generate harm.

When the story begins, Macbeth is an honoured general in the King of Scotland's army, returning from a hard-fought victory which has won him great praise. But on the way he and another general, Banquo, meet three witches, 'the weird sisters', who prophesy that Macbeth himself will become King. From that moment, the seed of evil that is in Macbeth, and the ambition, take root and begin to grow. After the briefest of struggles with his conscience, and incited to the crime by his wife, he butchers the King, the innocent and holy Duncan, whilst he is visiting Macbeth's castle.

The sovereignty falls on Macbeth. But he does not feel secure. The witches predicted that Banquo's heirs would finally ascend to the throne. For safety, Macbeth has two killers cut Banquo's throat. The same night he gives a royal banquet to the Court at which he sees the ghost of Banquo, stained in blood. Macbeth's terror makes the Court, who cannot see the phantom, think the King is mad.

The chain of horror goes on. Macbeth has Lady Macduff and her children murdered — for the witches, whom he has seen again, have told him to beware of Macduff, a chieftain.

Conscience and fear now begin to torture him. Lady Macbeth, firm before, is also haunted by their crimes, and sleepwalks through the night, forever washing her hands to rid them of blood. They are a king and queen of nightmares, pursued by guilt as though by the Furies.

In England, meanwhile, Macduff has joined forces with Duncan's son, Malcolm, who is raising an army there against Macbeth who prepares to defend his castle. The news comes to him that his Queen, in madness and remorse, has committed suicide. He is by then, to use Kenneth Tynan's words 'a cornered thug'. Macduff kills him; Malcolm becomes King.

Peter Hall, who has directed *Macbeth* for the National Theatre and the Royal Shakespeare Company, says: 'It isn't about "should I or should I not do a murder?". The question is never asked. It is about what happens when I *do* do a murder: the evil which is released . . . the way evil breeds evil, blood breeds blood, badness breeds badness.'

The blood-soaked story is redeemed by the speed and power of the narrative and a central character who, though a murderer of awesome brutality, possesses a fascinating mind full of dark poetic introspection. Schlegel writes of the play: 'Since Aeschylus, nothing so grand and terrible has ever been composed.'

Antony and Cleopatra
(written 1606/7)

ANTONY AND CLEOPATRA is perhaps the richest play about love in the English language, an epic flood of sensuality and despair. Herbert Farjeon says: 'It reels with passion — not the sweet young boy-and-girl passion of *Romeo and Juliet*, but violent, overstrained, suspicious, recriminative, adult passion, just past its prime. . . . It begins magnificently. It goes on magnificently. It ends most magnificently of all.' Coleridge writes that 'of all Shakespeare's plays the most wonderful is *Antony and Cleopatra*'.

On stage, it can be an unforgettable experience. Yet it is rarely seen. One of the reasons theatre directors are wary of it may be the part of Cleopatra, arguably the most demanding female role of all, and difficult to cast. Most people have a romantic picture of her which is not Shakespeare's. To him, to quote Farjeon again: 'She is riggish. She is vain. She is vulgar. She is cruel. She is cowardly. She is a born commander. She is a born slave. She is innately faithful. She is innately deceitful.'

Cleopatra's 'infinite variety' calls for, as well, an actress who can bring together a sense of majesty, great vocal control and range, and ripe sexual attraction. A. C. Bradley stresses her wantonness: 'She cannot see an ambassador, scarcely even a messenger, without desiring to bewitch him. . . . Even when death is close at hand, she imagines his touch as a lover's.'

The play itself reflects the power of its two main characters by spanning the entire Mediterranean world. The text is full of images of this vastness: of orbs, spheres, planets, sun, moon. The drama shows domestic passion

61

against a panoramic public setting. Antony is described as 'The triple pillar of the world transform'd/Into a strumpet's fool'. He has allowed his passion for Cleopatra to over-whelm his great gifts as a soldier and leader. His taste for riot and excess has taken over and he has become a libertine.

Even in disaster, however, he still manages to keep the devotion of those in the army who are closest to him. Enobarbus — to whom Shakespeare gives lines that create for the audience Antony's nobility and Cleopatra's fascina-tion almost as much as the protagonists themselves do by their own words and actions — deserts Antony in disgust. But it breaks Enobarbus' heart, and he dies.

The actual plot of the play is simplicity itself. Antony, holding power in Egypt for Rome, and wishing to patch up his relationship with Octavius Caesar, separates from Cleopatra and marries Octavius' sister. He then deserts her to return to Cleopatra. As a result, war breaks out, Octavius defeats the two lovers, and they kill themselves.

Though Antony and Cleopatra are figures of immense political power, they are also self-destructive, undeviating sensualists, feeling the world well lost for love. So it is not like Shakespeare, who was no hedonist, to regard them with the sympathy he does. Ivor Brown writes of this: 'Shakespeare was, on the whole, a temperate man, careful of his money, nervous that his sensibility might betray him, afraid of his passion. But on this occasion he stripped moderation from his mind.'

In the end, Antony and Cleopatra win our pity because they both, separately, accept death with courage and nobility. Their passion for one another is transcendent, looking beyond death.

King Lear
(written c1607)

Of all Shakespeare's plays, KING LEAR is the most awe-inspiring. Its characters seem powerless against an unrelenting destiny. But though they move towards betrayal and torture, madness and death, with no apparent hope of release, a number of them gain in strength and dignity.

'The story is the hardest, cruellest, most uncompromising message that any dramatist has ever presented to his audience', writes Trevor Nunn, who within eight years directed *King Lear* twice for the Royal Shakespeare Company.

The play is set in pre-Christian Britain. But it has a curious timelessness. It could be the dawn of the world, it could be now.

Lear, a great king, considering himself too old to hold power, decides to divide his kingdom between his three daughters. He tells them that the one who loves him most will get the largest share. The elder daughters, Goneril and Regan, declare with overblown flattery that they love him extravagantly. Cordelia, the youngest and his favourite, answers that she loves him simply, with a daughter's love. Lear, furious, disowns her, and banishes the Earl of Kent for trying to prevent him. Cordelia leaves Britain to marry the King of France.

Lear is now without power. But he remains autocratic and demanding. Goneril and Regan, impatient with him but holding the kingdom between them, bait him cruelly. Their ingratitude begins to affect his mind. He rushes out into the night with his Fool, and they are caught in a merciless storm. Here Lear defies the thunder and pelting rain, strips off his clothes, and stands half-naked to the weather. At this moment he is 'without possessions of any kind. We have watched All become Nothing — or Nothing become All' (Trevor Nunn). It is the beginning of his process of self-discovery, to continue in madness, 'cut to the brains'.

News of her father's agony brings Cordelia back to Britain with a French force to avenge his wrongs. But in a battle she and Lear are made prisoners.

Later, the battle swings the other way, but orders have been given for Lear and Cordelia to be killed. It is too late to save Cordelia; she is carried in by Lear, dead. The King dies with her in his arms, but not before he has at last recognised Kent who, in disguise, has with loving care attended his 'sad steps' from the first.

That is the tragedy's main plot. But what happens to Lear is subtly counterpointed through the play by what happens to the Earl of Gloucester, unlike Lear an earthy rationalist. He too rejects one of his children, in his case a son. He too suffers appalling injury: he is brutally blinded. And at the last he too finds love and comfort in the child he rejected. In one superb scene, full of tragic irony, Lear and Gloucester meet; the King is mad and Gloucester blind: the words they speak are amongst the most haunting in dramatic literature.

King Lear is believed to have been the last of the great tragedies. In 1681 it was altered and a notorious happy end added by Nahum Tate — the seventeenth-century dramatist. This falsified text was acted for the next 150 years and more. Charles Lamb, who saw Tate's version, and knew it for what it was, nevertheless writes famously: 'The Lear of Shakespeare cannot be acted . . . they might more easily propose to personate the Satan of Milton upon a stage, or one of Michael Angelo's terrible figures.' He had never seen the real play.

More recently, there have been ample opportunities to

do so. Remarkable modern productions, and performances in the name part, have vividly imprinted the image of *King Lear* on the imagination of the twentieth century.

Timon of Athens
(written 1607/8)

It has been questioned whether TIMON OF ATHENS was actually written by Shakespeare. There have been theories that it was only a draft by him, redone later by a second, unknown, hand. But it is believed now that the play is his, and unfinished.

Why the text is incomplete can only be guessed at. Shakespeare could have been suffering a nervous breakdown. Or perhaps he became merely bored. But Ivor Brown, writing of the many venereal images in the play, says: 'Bored? No, he was boiling with abhorrence.'

The plot can be briefly told. Timon is a rich Greek patrician whose prodigality is so extreme he is the patron and host of everybody in Athens. But because of his generosity his money goes. His friends refuse to help him, and they melt away. Timon changes utterly. He leaves Athens for a cave in the woods, and lives there a hermit and misanthrope, hating and railing against mankind.

Critical opinion of *Timon* over the last 200 years has reflected changing attitudes in each era. In the eighteenth century, treating the play as Neo-Classical tragedy, Doctor Johnson is moralistic: 'The catastrophe affords a very powerful warning against that ostentatious liberality which scatters bounty, but confers no benefits, and buys flattery, but not friendship.' At the beginning of the nineteenth century, the Romantic movement which produced Byron and Shelley was strong: 'Timon is tormented' says Hazlitt 'with the perpetual contrast between things and appearances, between the fresh, tempting outside and the rottenness within.' In our own time, the play's extreme pessimism can be accepted: G. Wilson Knight writes, 'We are given no chance to sentimentalise Timon's hate . . . it is thus not a cold vacuum of the soul but a dynamic force, possessing purpose and direction.'

Between the time *Timon* was composed, and its revival at Drury Lane by Edmund Kean nearly two centuries later, records show only one professional production of the play as it was written — in Dublin in 1761. All the others were more or less falsifications, even Kean's. But Samuel Phelps' performances in the mid-nineteenth century were in the van of a number of true revivals. Few though have wooed the public from a distaste for the play's ghastly declamations against lust and ingratitude.

Despite that, Ivor Brown finds this rhetoric 'in its own macabre way, superb. For its torrents of world-loathing and summoning of doom there can be nothing like it in English literature, not even in Shakespeare's masterpieces.'

Coriolanus
(written c1607/8)

The time is about 490 BC. The place is in and around Rome when it was barbaric, small, and constantly threatened by marauding tribes. Caius Marcius, a proud Roman and a superb warrior, fights with great valour against the Volscian tribes at Corioli, near to Rome — so much so that he is given the title CORIOLANUS.

He is acclaimed as Rome's saviour, the hero of the people. But after a time they begin to hate him for the very qualities that made him their idol: his fearless and unbending nature, his arrogance, his belief that he is gifted above the common man, a god. When he seeks the Consulship, the people rise against him and banish him from Rome.

Returning hate with hate, Coriolanus wanders into the wilderness and is befriended by his one-time enemies, the Volscians, and their leader, Tullus Aufidius, whom he now joins to attack Rome.

Together they bring Rome to her knees. At the gates, in a powerful scene that has been the subject of many paintings, Coriolanus is begged by his mother, wife, and small son to spare his own city. Their pleading is too strong for him. He agrees to what they ask. Filled with rage, the Volscians kill him.

The play is Shakespeare's most political drama, and it has been mounted at various times to reflect very different political attitudes. The Victorians staged it as if its central character were an Imperialist. In 1933, at the Comédie Française, he was shown as a stainless hero: Parisian mobs rioted at every performance and the production had to close. On the other hand, Bertolt Brecht, a confirmed Marxist, wrote a version for the Berliner Ensemble which, though in general faithful to Shakespeare, contained significant changes that indicate the people can do well without Coriolanus: the leader is not indispensable.

Certainly there is room in Shakespeare's text for stressing the rights of the people over their leaders, as there is for stressing exactly the opposite. There is, too, the interesting contrast between Coriolanus, a saviour in war but an embarrassment in peace, and the practised politician, Menenius, who is able to woo and calm the people and knows how to manipulate their Tribunes. Coriolanus, urged to flatter the people to win the Consulship, simply cannot do so.

The play was not popular in past centuries. But modern critics and audiences have admired it greatly for its ironies and exciting story. It is still, though, not loved. The nature of the central character lacks the restlessness and pain of an uncertain heart; he is of politics, not of poetry. He has been described as 'a demented aristocrat . . . a cheerless and unattractive snob' by Wyndham Lewis, and as an 'incorrigible boy' by Granville-Barker. T. S. Eliot, however, thinks the play 'Shakespeare's most assured artistic success.'

Pericles
(written c1608)

PERICLES, Prince of Tyre, could be by others as well as Shakespeare. It is grouped as a romance, with *The Tempest, The Winter's Tale*, and *Cymbeline*. These are, superficially, like fairytales. People are shipwrecked and miraculously saved, gods and goddesses appear in visions, princesses who seem dead are restored to life, all usually ends happily.

The story of *Pericles* is of an epic journey, both a real and a spiritual one, by the Prince of Tyre in his quest for a wife. Presenting this as chorus figure is John Gower whose fourteenth-century poem was Shakespeare's main source. The play's subject is love.

Pericles first wishes to marry King Antiochus' daughter but finds out that she is the lover of her own father. Sickened at this incest, he leaves Antioch and sails to Tarsus. Here he rescues the city from famine, earning the gratitude of its governor, Cleon, and his wife, Dionyza. But, menaced by King Antiochus, he sails away, is shipwrecked, and thrown on an unknown shore where he is befriended by that country's King, Simonides.

Pericles wins Simonides' daughter, Thaisa, as his wife. He returns to Antioch with her after hearing that its wicked King is dead. But on the journey Thaisa gives birth to a daughter during a storm at sea, and dies. Pericles places her body in a casket which is thrown into the ocean. The casket floats to shore at Ephesus, and Thaisa is brought back to life. Convinced that her husband is drowned, she becomes a votaress of the goddess Diana.

Pericles, grief-stricken at the loss of Thaisa, gives his baby daughter Marina — so named because she was born at sea — to the care of Cleon and Dionysa at Tarsus.

Time passes. The Princess Marina grows beautiful, and Cleon and Dionyza, filled with jealousy of her beauty compared to their own daughter, plan for her to be killed. But she is abducted by pirates, and sold to a brothel-keeper at Mytelene where her goodness enables her to remain a virgin.

Pericles, crushed by the loss of his daughter and his wife, arrives at Mytelene, meets his daughter again, and is restored to happiness. The goddess Diana appears to him in a vision and bids him go to Ephesus, where he finds Thaisa. There is a joyful family reunion.

Though Ben Jonson called *Pericles* 'some mouldy tale' and grumbled at its success, the play is extraordinary for a quality which is, at once, childlike, majestic, and metaphysical. John Wain writes: 'The truth it aims at is not the truth of realistic character-portrayal or closely observed and probable action. It is the truth of fable, which expresses things close to the heart of man by means of symbolic action . . . *Pericles* is a first step in the art of blending romance with a drama of pageantry, masques and stage illusions.' Terry Hands, who directed a remarkable Royal Shakespeare Company production, says: 'The allegory is conveyed by the simplest emotions: grief, happiness, fathers and daughters, husbands and wives. For those who wish it there is metaphor. For those who wish it there is fairytale. Either can be ignored without detriment to the experience, or both accepted.'

Cymbeline
(written 1609/10)

CYMBELINE, one of Shakespeare's romances, is a difficult and curious play with a convoluted plot. Poorly presented it can seem inept. Well staged it can hold an audience enthralled. Many theatre directors find a challenge in its sometimes absurd situations. Most actresses long to appear as the heroine, Imogen, whose character is a marvellous blend of courage, resource, rashness, and passion.

The story, though concerned with lustful deceptions, murder, and loss of faith between husband and wife, is in a sense a fairytale — as are the other romances, *Pericles, The Winter's Tale*, and *The Tempest*.

Cymbeline is King of a half-legendary, pagan Britain at the time of the Roman occupation. His two sons are lost, abducted as babies twenty years earlier by a Lord. His daughter, Imogen, expected by the Queen to marry her son by a former husband, has without the King's consent married Posthumus Leonatus, poor, but 'most prais'd, most lov'd'.

Banished by the King, Posthumus leaves Imogen and goes to friends in Rome, where he wagers with an Italian,

Iachimo, that she is a faithful wife. Iachimo sails to England, finds that Imogen is faithful, but hides in her bedchamber, and when she is asleep slips her bracelet off her arm and notices a mole on her left breast. He returns to Rome and, with this evidence, persuades Posthumus she has been unfaithful. Posthumus, distraught, sends orders to his servant, attending Imogen in London, to kill her.

Imogen in innocence of this leaves the Court for Milford Haven where Posthumus has written he will meet her. But she learns there of his plans to kill her, and in anguish wanders away into the Welsh mountains.

There, disguised as a boy, she has many adventures. She makes friends with two people who, unknown to her, are her brothers, Cymbeline's lost sons. In one poignant scene they believe her, the boy stranger they have grown to love, to be dead. They speak over her body the immortal lyric beginning 'Fear no more the heat o' the sun . . .' In another scene, she wakes beside a headless body which she supposes is her husband (it is, in fact, the Queen's son who had come to rape her and been killed by the brothers), holds it like a lover in her arms, and speaks in love, terror, and hate of her circumstances.

All ends happily after the Romans land to obtain unpaid tribute, and are beaten in battle. For Posthumus, who has returned from Rome and fought valiantly with the Britons, discovers Iachimo's deception. And Cymbeline is reconciled with his daughter, her marriage, and his two lost sons.

The last act, which contains a splendidly elaborate Masque of Jupiter descending mounted on an eagle, is sometimes thought to be stagey trash. But Bernard Shaw, who was fascinated by the play's glories and failings, wrote an entire alternative ending, saying: 'I shall not press my version on managers if they have the courage and good sense to present the original word-for-word as Shakespeare left it.'

John Wain regards *Cymbeline* as Shakespeare's 'most avant-garde work', and says its verse has a 'strange, haunting rhythm . . . that remains in our minds longest when everything else fades'.

A special understanding of the play is shown by John Masefield. He writes: 'It is clearly Shakespeare's scheme to show craft working upon an insufficient faith for wicked ends, and being defeated when almost successful by something simple and instinctive in human nature . . . *Cymbeline* is throughout coloured with romance, with the praise of simple country life, and with that strange touching late-Shakespearean tenderness for the thing long-lost, beautifully recovered before the end.'

The Winter's Tale
(written 1611)

THE WINTER'S TALE, *Pericles, Cymbeline,* and *The Tempest*, contain 'a world of meanings and wonder withdrawn within itself like the late quartets of Beethoven' (A. L. Rowse).

Trevor Nunn, who directed *The Winter's Tale* in a season of late plays for the Royal Shakespeare Company, says that they 'reconcile the paradox of man; they do not idealize the human condition, the beast is there all right, so also is the angel . . . They are not naturalistic plays, their imagery is dreamlike and fantastic. They are parables, they work both as fables and allegories.'

The Winter's Tale can be said to be about the effect of Time, both as enemy and friend, destroyer and renewer. There is a wide gap of sixteen years between the first part, which shows the betrayals of middle age, and the second, when children have grown into young lovers, and the characters become happy, and blessed. Both sides of the play are reflected in the Old Shepherd's words: 'Thou mett'st with things dying . . . I with things new-born.'

The first part of the story tells how Leontes, King of Sicilia, suddenly and irrationally suspects his wife Hermione of adultery with his friend, the King of Bohemia. Leontes condemns Hermione and commands that her new-born daughter be taken to some desolate place 'quite out of our dominions' and left there.

Soon after, the Oracle of Apollo declares to the Court that 'Hermione is chaste . . . Leontes a jealous tyrant' who will 'live without an heir' if he does not find his lost daughter. This is immediately followed by the death of their little son Mamillius and the apparent death of Hermione. In an agony of repentance, Leontes goes into mourning.

Hermione's baby, Perdita, left alone on the coast of Bohemia, is found by two shepherds who cherish her. Sixteen years pass. In the second part of the play, it is springtime. Perdita is now a beautiful girl who believes herself to be just a shepherdess, as do her friends. But she is loved by, and loves, Florizel, the son of Leontes' one-time friend, the King of Bohemia, who thinks her too poorly-born to become Princess. She and Florizel are advised by a Sicilian Lord, who is with the King of Bohemia, to run away to Leontes' Court. Here it is discovered that Perdita, now married to Florizel, is Leontes' lost daughter. Leontes is reconciled to the King of Bohemia. And to everyone's joy Hermione is revealed to be still living.

Anthony Burgess has an interesting thought about the early performances of *The Winter's Tale*. He writes: 'If, as seems likely, Perdita's part was doubled by the boy-actor who took Leontes' son Mamillius, who dies early in the play, then we have a resurrection of deep significance for the man Shakespeare. Hamnet [his only son] died, but a loved daughter takes his place, and their lineaments are the same.' Shakespeare had two daughters, Susanna and Judith.

The Tempest
(written 1611)

THE TEMPEST, one of the masterpieces of all literature, is also the most enigmatic of Shakespeare's works, and can be theatrically unsatisfying. A great deal of its substance seems deliberately hidden beneath the surface. People see in the central character, Prospero — who possesses a power of magic which he finally relinquishes — the figure of Shakespeare himself saying farewell to his own genius.

In the centuries since *The Tempest* was first performed, writers have been drawn to it constantly, using it in a remarkable number of ways. Its themes have been recreated in operas, films and poems, and made the basis of philosophical and theological works.

The plot, which is of storm and shipwreck, and the survival of men on an island, was without much doubt inspired by the actual adventures of the crew of a British ship, *Sea Adventure*, bound for Virginia in 1609. Caught in a storm and partially wrecked, her mariners landed on an island thought to be inhabited by demons, and found it beautiful and healthy.

Reports of this adventure reached England at the time *The Tempest* was written and were much commented upon. Shakespeare certainly read the letters and pamphlets about the episode, for he used factual details from them in his play.

The story tells how Prospero, usurped as Duke of Milan by his brother Antonio, and cast adrift in 'a rotten carcass of a boat' with his little daughter Miranda twelve years before the action begins, now lives with her on an island. He is served by a spirit, Ariel, and an earth and sea monster, Caliban.

Using magic, Prospero raises a storm, and by ship-wrecking his brother Antonio, together with Alonso King of Naples, Alonso's brother Sebastian and son Ferdinand, and other lords and seamen, brings them to the island and, unknown to them, into his power.

Whilst they are there, Sebastian plots to kill his brother so as to become King of Naples; and the Court jester and a drunken butler are persuaded by Caliban to try to seize the island from Prospero, for Caliban tells them it is his. But Prospero prevents these plans, is reconciled with his brother, gives his blessing to the love that has grown between Miranda and Ferdinand, sets Ariel free, and pardons Caliban.

Despite this happy conclusion, *The Tempest* seems not to have the optimism of Shakespeare's other romances. In these — *The Winter's Tale, Cymbeline*, and *Pericles* — sin and suffering are, at the end, reconciled with the goodness in man. In *The Tempest* there is a note of pessimism.

Prospero is a great magician who can raise storms, darken the sun at noontide, and raise the dead to life. But, writes Anne Barton, 'What his art cannot do is the thing which ultimately matters most; he can never change the nature and inclinations of the human heart. He cannot *make* Ferdinand and Miranda fall in love, nor guarantee the happiness of their union. He has no way of forcing the men who plot against him to be good. Caliban cannot be civilised or made grateful.'

In the end Prospero breaks his magic staff, and drowns

75

his book of power deep in the sea. He will, he says, go back to Milan 'where every third thought shall be my grave'.

Henry VIII
(written c1613)

Many commentators now believe that HENRY VIII is the result of a collaboration between Shakespeare and John Fletcher, despite there being no direct evidence of this. They were, though, at the time, the chief dramatists of the same company and had already jointly written *The Two Noble Kinsmen* according to the 1634 quarto edition of that play.

Henry VIII tells its story in a series of somewhat disconnected but vividly theatrical episodes. It is set before and during the King's passion for Anne Boleyn. He is in his early forties, lusty, impulsive, worshipped by his people, a hunter, wrestler, poet, musician — the complete man, and at the peak of his strength. The play shows Wolsey's arrogance and fall; Cranmer's Protestant convictions and their use by the King for his own ends; Queen Katharine's nobility when divorced and abandoned; and, briefly, the first meeting between the King and the young Anne Boleyn who, at the play's conclusion, gives birth to the daughter destined to become the greatest Tudor of all, Elizabeth.

Of all Shakespeare's histories, *Henry VIII* is the one that chronicles matters nearest to the dramatist's own time. Henry had died only about 65 years before the play was first performed. Almost everything in it happened. The only changes are in the succession of events and certain people.

To some extent, the story is dominated by the theme of the fall of greatness — Katharine and Wolsey both lose their high authority, Buckingham his head. But the play is mainly liked for its scenes of celebration: the coronation of Anne Boleyn, and the Royal christening at which Cranmer, holding the infant Elizabeth in his arms, foretells the glorious future of England under her rule, bringing 'Peace, Plenty, Love, Truth'.

Because of these opportunities for patriotic pageantry, *Henry VIII* is often given with great splendour when there is national rejoicing, and has twice been presented at the time of coronations: in 1727 for the crowning of George II, and in 1953 for the crowning of Elizabeth II.

G. Wilson Knight writes: 'If in *The Tempest* Shakespeare gives us a comprehensive and inclusive statement of his own further spiritual adventures, in *Henry VIII* he has gone yet further, directly relating those adventures to the religion of his day and the nation of his birth.'

Who's Who and Select Bibliography

AUDEN, W. H. *16, 34, 36*
1907-1973. Poet, verse dramatist, essayist. Work includes essays on Shakespeare's characters.

BARTON, Anne *56, 75*
Fellow of New College, Oxford, since 1974. Author of *Shakespeare and the Idea of the Play* (Chatto, 1962).

BARTON, John *34, 50*
Born 1928. Associate director of Royal Shakespeare Company. Director of plays. Adaptor of Shakespeare texts.

BRADLEY, A. C *61*
1851-1935. Fellow of Balliol College, Oxford. Literary critic. Author of *Shakespearean Tragedy* (London, 1904) and *Oxford Lectures on Poetry* (London, 1911).

BRAHMS, Caryl *12*
Novelist, journalist specialising in theatre comment, ballet critic, scriptwriter for radio, TV, films.

BROOK, Peter *28*
Born 1925. Associate director of Royal Shakespeare Company. Play, opera, film director. Author.

BROWN, Ivor *10, 57, 62, 65, 66*
1891-1974. Journalist, critic, editor of *The Observer*. Author of *Shakespeare* (Collins, 1949); *Shakespeare in His Time* (Nelson, 1960); *How Shakespeare Spent the Day* (Bodley Head, 1963); *Shakespeare and His World* (Lutterworth, 1964); *The Women in Shakespeare's Life* (Bodley Head, 1968); *Shakespeare and the Actors* (Bodley Head, 1970).

BROWN, John Russell *31, 45*
Born 1923. Professor of English at Sussex University. Director of plays. An associate director of the National Theatre. Author of *Shakespeare's Dramatic Style* (Heinemann Educational, 1973); *Shakespeare and His Comedies* (Methuen, 1957); *Free Shakespeare* (Heinemann Educational, 1974).

BURGESS, Anthony *13, 15, 17, 29, 30, 73*
Born 1917. Novelist, critic, journalist, biographer, scriptwriter. Wrote novel on Shakespeare, *Nothing Like the Sun* (Heinemann, 1964) and a biography, *Shakespeare* (Cape, 1970).

CHURCHILL, Winston *14, 18*
1874-1965. Statesman, historian. Wrote a 12-volume history *The Second World War* (Cassell).

COLERIDGE, Samuel Taylor *16, 50, 54, 61*
1772-1834. Poet, critic, philosopher. Wrote essays, notes, and gave over forty lectures on Shakespeare's work.

COOKMAN, A. V. *10*
1895-1962. Drama critic of *The Times* for nearly 20 years. Shakespeare scholar.

ELIOT, T. S. *68*
1889-1965. American-born poet, playwright, critic. Author of essays, *Hamlet and his Problems*, and a controversial essay on *Othello*.

EMPSON, William *35*
Born 1906. Professor of English Literature, Sheffield University, 1953-1971,

now Emeritus. Poet. Has published many books of poems, and a volume on *The Structure of Complex Words* (Chatto and Windus, 1951).

FARJEON, Herbert *12, 61*
1889-1945. Author, playwright, critic, journalist, theatre manager. Edited *The Shakespeare Journal*, and *The Nonesuch Shakespeare*.

GOETHE, Johann Wolfgang *52*
1749-1832. German poet, author, critic, dramatist, scientist, philosopher. Work influenced by Shakespeare. Wrote adaptation of *Romeo and Juliet*.

GRANVILLE-BARKER, Harley *68*
1877-1946. Playwright, critic, actor, director. Author of *Prefaces to Shakespeare* (Batsford, 1958); *A Companion to Shakespeare Studies* (C.U.P., 1945).

HALL, Edward *41*
c. 1498-1547. Tudor historian. Author of the chronicles, *The Union of the Two Noble and Illustr Famelies of Lancastre and York*. Shakespeare almost certainly used these for his earlier history plays.

HALL, Peter *21, 34, 42, 48, 60*
Born 1930. Founded Royal Shakespeare Company. Director of National Theatre since 1973. Director of plays, films, operas.

HALL, Stuart *53*
Born 1932. Director of Centre for Cultural Studies, Birmingham University. Sociologist, author, critic, broadcaster.

HANDS, Terry *70*
Born 1941. Co-artistic director with Trevor Nunn of the Royal Shakespeare Company since 1978; Royal Shakespeare Company associate director 1967-77. Consultant director at the Comédie Française 1975-77. Director of plays, operas.

HAZLITT, William *32, 39, 58, 66*
1778-1830. Critic, essayist. Wrote famous series of essays *The Characters of Shakespeare's Plays*.

JOHNSON, Samuel *13, 15, 39, 54, 65*
1709-1784. Critic, essayist, scholar, lexicographer. Edited 8-volume text of Shakespeare's plays with annotations and famous preface.

JONSON, Ben *69*
1572-1637. Poet, playwright. Shakespeare's fellow-dramatist and friend. Wrote poem to Shakespeare in First Folio.

KNIGHT, G. Wilson *58, 66, 77*
Born 1897. Professor of English Literature, Leeds University 1956-1962, now Emeritus. Theatre director, broadcaster on Shakespeare, essayist. Author of many books on Shakespeare including, most recently, *Shakespeare's Dramatic Challenge* (Croom Helm, 1977).

LAMB, Charles *64*
1775-1834. Essayist, and author with his sister Mary of *Tales from Shakespeare*. His many essays include *Shakespeare's Tragedies*.

LEWIS, Wyndham *68*
1884-1957. American-born painter, critic, novelist.

MARX, Karl *38*
1818-1883. German philosopher and theorist; laid the foundation of modern Communism.

MASEFIELD, John *13, 20, 25, 26, 27, 72*
1878-1967. Novelist, poet. Works include *Shakespeare* (London 1911 and 1954) and *Shakespeare and the Spiritual Life* (O.U.P., 1924). Poet Laureate.

MAUGHAM, W. Somerset *16*
1874-1965. Author, dramatist.

NUNN, Trevor *10, 63, 64, 72*
Born 1940. Director of Royal Shakespeare Company since 1968; co-director with Terry Hands since 1978. Director of plays.

OLIVIER, Laurence, 49
Born 1907. Actor, director of plays and films. Founded National Theatre Company at Old Vic. Has played all the major Shakespeare roles. Has made three Shakespeare films: *Henry V, Richard III, Othello.*
PEPYS, Samuel *30*
1633-1703. Diarist and inveterate playgoer. Kept record of London life for nine years during Restoration, including lively comment on plays and players.
RALEIGH, Walter *50*
1552-1618. Elizabethan nobleman and adventurer. Author of a *History of the World.*
ROSSITER, A. P. *24, 51*
1904-1957. Fellow of Jesus College, Cambridge, from 1945. Author of *English Drama from Early Times to the Elizabethans* (Hutchinson, 1950).
ROWSE, A. L. *41, 72*
Born 1903. Fellow of All Souls, Oxford, and Royal Society of Literature. Author, critic, biographer, lecturer. Author of many books on Elizabethan England including *William Shakespeare: a Biography* (Macmillan, 1963).
SCHLEGEL, August Wilhelm *60*
1767-1845. German scholar, critic, poet. Translated 13 of Shakespeare's plays.
SCOFIELD, Paul *50*
Born 1922. Actor. Has played many Shakespeare roles including Hamlet, King Lear, Macbeth, Timon.
SHAW, Bernard *11, 40-41, 43, 51, 53-4, 56, 71*
1856-1950. Dramatist, essayist, critic, socialist. Noted theatre and music critic. His reviews in the 1890s of Shakespeare's plays were highly controversial.
TILLYARD, E. M. W. *26*
1889-1962. Master of Jesus College, Cambridge, 1945-1959. Critic, essayist, lecturer, author. His many books on Shakespeare include: *Shakespeare's History Plays* (Chatto and Windus, 1944); *Shakespeare's Last Plays* (Chatto and Windus, 1938); *Shakespeare's Problem Plays* (Chatto and Windus, 1950).
TREVELYAN, G. M. *19*
1876-1962. Master of Trinity College, Cambridge, 1940-1951. Historian, biographer. Author of *English Social History Survey of Six Centuries* (Longman).
TYNAN, Kenneth *9, 60*
Born 1927. Critic, essayist, journalist. Literary manager of the National Theatre, 1963-1973.
WAIN, John *27, 58-59, 69-70, 72*
Born 1925. Professor of Poetry, Oxford, since 1973. Novelist, biographer, essayist, reviewer, broadcaster. Books include *The Living World of Shakespeare* (Macmillan, 1964).
WILLIAMS, Clifford *27-8, 34*
Born 1926. Associate director of Royal Shakespeare Company. Director of plays.
WILSON, John Dover *40, 50*
1881-1969. Author, critic. Editor of *The New Cambridge Shakespeare.* Wrote many critical studies and books on Shakespeare including *The Essential Shakespeare* (C.U.P., 1932); *What Happens in Hamlet* (C.U.P., 1935, 1951); *The Fortunes of Falstaff* (C.U.P., 1943). Theorist on Shakespeare's texts.